the GOLDEN THREAD

the GOLDEN THREAD

The Ageless Wisdom of
the Western Mystery Traditions

JOSCELYN GODWIN

QUEST

BOOKS

Theosophical Publishing House
Wheaton, Illinois • Chennai, India

Quest Books
Theosophical Publishing House
P.O. Box 270 • Wheaton, IL 60189-0270

www.questbooks.net

Cover image: *Philosopher with Flask,* illustration from the First Treatise of *Splendor Solis.* © British Library Board. All rights reserved. Harley .3489 f4.
Cover design, book design, and typesetting by Dan Doolin

A limited clothbound edition of *The Golden Thread* (ISBN 978-0-9712044-5-4) is also available from Dominion Press, P.O. Box 129, Waterbury Center, VT 05766 USA. E-mail: dominion@pshift.com

Library of Congress Cataloging-in-Publication Data

Godwin, Joscelyn.
The golden thread: the ageless wisdom of the Western mystery traditions / Joscelyn Godwin; foreword by Richard Smoley.
p. cm.
ISBN-13: 978-0-8356-0860-2
ISBN-10: 0-8356-0860-3
1. Mysteries, Religious.   I. Title.
BL610.G625   2007
135—dc22   2007008418

Printed in the United States of America

5   4   3   2   1   *   07   08   09   10   11

Contents

Foreword

"Wisdom crieth without, she uttereth her voice in the streets," we read in a book of ancient wisdom. "I have called, and ye refused; I have stretched out my hand, and no man regardeth" (Prov. 1:20,24). Although we in the modern (or postmodern) world are fond of congratulating ourselves on our advancements, it would be hard to read these verses without observing how little has changed since the remote time when they were written. Wisdom, it seems, is always crying in the streets and is never, or rarely, heard. This fact is, to all appearances, as much a part of the human condition as birth, death, suffering, and work.

Even in this context, it would appear that the fate of wisdom in the West has been an unusually dark one. What has survived of it has done so under almost unimaginably inhospitable circumstances. Consider: sixteen hundred years ago, a persecuted faith that suddenly became the state religion of the Roman Empire jumped at the chance to avenge the ills that had been visited upon it, suppressing all its rivals, closing their schools, burning their libraries, and chasing their philosophers out of the country. When, not long after, the empire collapsed (partly thanks to the new faith, which had diverted the empire's resources toward persecuting heretics rather than combatting external foes), the event ushered in centuries of oblivion, an age when, in Western Europe at any rate, even the most learned men could scarcely write a grammatical sentence.

Centuries later, as this ill-starred civilization began to lift its head out of ignorance, it found itself in the clutches of the same church, which, claiming spiritual hegemony over the entire planet, tried to institute what historian Paul Johnson has called a "total society." It was the first attempt at totalitarianism as we know it: the church claimed the right not only to external allegiance but to control over the inmost thoughts of its subjects. If in these times the same organization proved to be a protector of the ancient wisdom almost as often as it was a persecutor, we can take it only as proof that there is nothing totally good or totally evil under the sun.

When, further centuries later, the hegemony of the church began to wane, it was supplanted by a new religion or pseudoreligion, one that denied the existence of any reality other than the purely physical and mechanical, and which sought to govern the life and behavior of humanity solely on the basis of physical laws (or on some interpretation of them). The only reality, says the new religion, is quantity; what cannot be weighed or measured or counted does not exist, or might as well not exist.

This is where we are today. If somewhere in all this, wisdom—or the love of wisdom, which is virtually the same thing—has survived, we can ascribe the fact only to the benevolence of some higher power, or, perhaps, to the hidden thirst of humanity, which longs for wisdom often even without knowing what it is longing for. We have also to give credit to the courage and prowess of a few individuals who are spread out so thinly over the centuries that it is no exaggeration to call their line a thread. Because this line is a precious one—very likely the most precious of all—it is also appropriate to call it a golden thread.

In this work, Joscelyn Godwin traces this golden thread from its origins in the eras of legend, when fact and myth shade into one another so that they are now indistinguishable, to the present day, when the thread of wisdom has, in its subtle and all but imperceptible way, has not only survived but has managed to nourish and sustain the civilization that has so often been its persecutor. If any tradition has been a better exemplar of the admonition "Love your enemies, bless them that curse you, do good to them that hate you, and pray for them which despitefully use you" (Matt. 5:44), I do not know of it. Even modern science, which now threatens to become a false and oppressive faith in its own right, owes its birth to this golden thread, which (as Professor Godwin shows) championed the inquiry into the workings of nature at a time when such inquiry was condemned as an unwarranted intrusion into the affairs of God.

It would be out of place for me here to attempt to describe either the history or the teachings of the Western esoteric tradition, since that is what Professor Godwin does so masterfully in this collection of essays. But it does seem appropriate to point out that in this tradition, knowledge is never merely "about" something. One cannot know something without experiencing it. Professor Godwin demonstrates this truth in an unusually subtle and powerful way. He explicates some of the most obscure and problematic ideas of the Western esoteric tradition—questions dealing with such matters as the survival of the soul after death, or the nature of entities on the subtle planes—in the context of a fascinating and illuminating story. I say this only to stress to readers that this work, in addition to its wealth of historical facts, also contains a treasure of rare and profound insights into the very substance of this tradition. Many of these insights appear in the endnotes, and I would strongly encourage readers not to overlook these.

The last chapter of this work, entitled "The End of the Thread?", asks whether this line of knowledge, which, both legend and scripture tell us, goes back to the very beginnings of the human race, is coming to an end now. If one looks at the surface of things, the answer almost seems foregone. But if we take a step back from the noise and anxiety of our time and see the matter in a wider view, I think it becomes reasonable to conclude that the golden thread is continuing and will continue as it always has. In fact the very existence of the book that you hold in your hands, and the work of the author who has created it, is testimony to that fact.

—RICHARD SMOLEY
Southampton, Massachusetts
February 2007

Preface

This book traces the thread of esoteric wisdom in the Western world, from classical antiquity to contemporary Europe and America. The arrangement is historical, but since this wisdom is timeless, each stage is perpetually present and a source of inspiration and action for today. Every chapter, therefore, makes reference to some aspect of contemporary life and immediate concern. This reflects the origin of the book in a series of fourteen articles written for *Lapis: The Inner Meaning of Contemporary Life,* a magazine associated with the Open Center in New York City. (*Lapis* is no longer published in print form, but is available in an on-line version: <www.lapis magazine.org>.)

The word *esoteric* refers to the inner aspect of a religion or philosophy, of which the outer aspect is *exoteric*. Thus Christianity once had its esoteric side in theosophy, the science of the knowledge of God; Judaism in Kabbalah; Islam in Sufism; Hinduism in the various yogas; Paganism in its Mysteries. These esoterisms were not for the majority of the faithful, but for those with sufficient interest, motivation, and capacity to benefit from them. Entry was through initiation, whereupon, under expert guidance, a few might embark on the lifelong and demanding quest for reality.

It is different today. There is a widespread thirst for a deeper dimension to life than the consumer society can provide, and for a better explanation of its mysteries than exoteric religion or materialistic science has to offer. This thirst accounts for the popular success of books and films that feature Gnostic and occult themes, and of conspiracy theories that claim that things are ordered quite differently—for good or ill—than the public is led to believe. If anyone wants to learn more, the secrets once imparted only to initiates are there on the bookshelves. The doors of the sanctuary are agape, but where are the hierophants, adepts, and sages whom one hoped to find there? Most of us seem to be thrown back on our own resources, lonely travelers among the ruined monuments of ancient mysteries. This book is offered by one such traveler, for the guidance and entertainment of others.

I would like to thank Ralph White, the editor of *Lapis*, who first invited me to treat the Western esoteric traditions in such a way that they would seem alive and relevant to his readers; Michael Moynihan of Dominion Press, who encouraged me to revise, annotate, and expand the original articles into book form; and Richard Smoley, my editor at Quest Books, for his wise advice and for kindly contributing a foreword.

—JOSCELYN GODWIN
Hamilton, New York
November 2006

1

The Prisca Theologia

When the Christian humanists of the Italian Renaissance studied the newly-discovered writings of the ancient philosophers, a new era opened in the self-image of Western civilization. It had long been taken for granted that, as the Bible relates, humanity toiled in ignorance and wickedness until the true God chose to reveal himself: to Noah, Abraham, Moses, and the Hebrew prophets, and finally in person as Jesus Christ. But these philosophers of antiquity, for all that they were pagans and polytheists, turned out to display a profound wisdom and a high spirituality. Some of them surely knew more than reason alone could explain: things that could only have come to them through divine revelation. The only reasonable conclusion was that God had not left his heathen children in total ignorance, but had revealed himself through their prophets (Zoroaster, Orpheus), priest-kings (Hermes

Trismegistus), and inspired philosophers (Pythagoras, Plato, Plotinus, Porphyry).

The bearer of this good news was an enigmatic character: Georgios Gemistos Plethon (c.1356–1450). A high official of the Byzantine Empire (or what was left of it), he lived in Mistra in the Peloponnese, the last holdout of Christian Byzantium in the Greek peninsula. His public mission was to attend the Council of Florence and Ferrara, convened in 1438–39 in the hope of reconciling the Greek (Orthodox) and the Roman (Catholic) churches.[1]

More privately, Gemistos met with the Florentine humanists,[2] to whom he explained his vision of a "primordial theology" (*prisca theologia*) periodically revealed to the pagan world. His lineage of the ancient illuminates began in Chaldea or Persia with Zoroaster, then moved to Thrace with Orpheus, whose disciple Aglaophemus was the link to Pythagoras and Plato. It was in honor of the latter that Gemistos had adopted the surname Plethon. The aged envoy made a powerful impression on his Italian hosts, and not least on Cosimo de' Medici, father of the famous dynasty. After his departure, Cosimo founded a Platonic Academy in his villa at Careggi, near Florence, and placed the scholar-priest Marsilio Ficino at its head. This became the center for the celebration, study, translation, and propagation of the "perennial philosophy" (*philosophia perennis*), the wisdom common to Jews, Christians, and pagans.

Gemistos could produce canonical scriptures for nearly all of his ancient theologians. To Zoroaster he ascribed the *Chaldean Oracles*; to Orpheus, the *Orphic Hymns*; to Pythagoras, the *Golden Verses*, and to Plato the *Republic*, *Laws*, and other works. To these the Florentine Platonists would add the *Corpus Hermeticum* and its author, who was confidently assumed to be the Egyptian philosopher-king Hermes Trismegistus (see chapter 2).[3]

In every case but Plato's, these attributions were mistaken. The *Chaldean Oracles, Orphic Hymns, Golden Verses,* and *Corpus Hermeticum* all date from the early centuries of the Common Era, whereas Pythagoras lived in the sixth century B.C., Zoroaster goodness knows when,[4] and Orpheus and Hermes perhaps never lived at all. The cold shower of modern philology has dispelled the dream of the ancient theologians, just as biblical scholarship has proved that Moses did not write the Torah (the first five books of the Bible). But this makes no difference to whatever intrinsic spiritual value they may contain.

Gemistos was an especial admirer of the *Chaldean Oracles*, whose origin as we now know it is the best-documented and the most provocative.[5] There was in Rome during the second century A.D. a family of astrologer-magicians called the Juliani, who like most of their profession passed as "Chaldeans." It would not be far wrong to compare them to the swamis and gurus of California, for in both places there was an openness to exotic cults. The senior Julianus, it appears, used his son as a trance-medium. While in trance, Julianus Jr. answered questions and uttered oracles that were believed to come from the gods. His material would have been utterly lost if the Neoplatonists had not preserved numerous fragments of it by quoting it in their works. From them it passed to Byzantium, where it was commented on by Michael Psellus (eleventh century), by Gemistos, and by the Italian Platonists, receiving monumental form in the edition by Francesco Patrizi (1593).

It would be correct to call the Juliani's activity "channeling," so long as the term is used in a precise and technical sense, not an emotional and derogatory one. The precise sense is this: the man or woman who speaks or writes the words in question does not claim to be their author, but to be acting as a channel for some other entity. The most famous and influential example is that of the Qur'an, for which Mohammed acted as channel, but never claimed authorship. In the case of the Oracles of the Juliani, they, like the Qur'an, were regarded as a divine revelation, not merely by cult members but by the greatest of Plato's commentators, Proclus.[6]

On the whole, the Chaldean system accords with the Hermetic, Orphic, and Platonic ones, as Proclus was at pains to demonstrate. Leaving aside its complicated theology, it sees the human soul as having come down from a divine state and become temporarily united with the body. Spiritual practice has the goal of restoring the soul to its original heritage.

A few of the *Oracles* suggest that the Juliani and their circle also had an idea of bodily transmutation as a means towards immortality. For example:

> The oracles of the Gods declare, that through purifying ceremonies, not the soul only, but bodies themselves become worthy of receiving much assistance and health: for (say they) the mortal vestment of bitter matter will, by this means, be preserved.[7]

Psellus, the Christian commentator, gives this explanation of the idea:

[The Oracle] exhorteth therefore, that we refine the Body (which he understands by the Dregs of Matter) by divine [acts], or that, being stripped, we raise it up to the Aether; or that we be exalted by God to a place Immaterial and Incorporeal, or Corporeal but Aethereal or Coelestial, which *Elias* the *Tisbite* attained; and before him, *Enoch*, being Translated from this Life into a more Divine Condition, not leaving the dregs of Matter, or their Body, in a Precipice; the Precipice is, as we said, the Terrestrial Region.[8]

As testified in the Bible, Enoch, Elijah, and Jesus left no physical body behind after their deaths.[9] The same was believed of the Virgin Mary from the fifth century onward, and in 1950 the Catholic church proclaimed it dogma. Although always skeptical when told what I must believe, I have no difficulty in principle with this concept, on which I will enlarge in chapter 2. It seems quite feasible that a person's physical body might be so transformed during life that it becomes indistinguishable from the subtle "radiant body." The soul then takes the body with it, wherever it goes after leaving earth.

There is reliable evidence that this has happened in modern times in the case of Tibetan adepts.[10] Eyewitness accounts support the tradition that adepts may achieve the "diamond body" during life. Then, within days after death, their physical body just disappears, leaving behind only the "vegetable" elements of hair and nails. A lesser phenomenon, well attested in Christendom, is that of saints' bodies that remain uncorrupted, sometimes for centuries. Evidently there is a whole science here, studied in ancient

Egypt and Tibet but temporarily in abeyance because of the limits of the Western imagination. Theoretical physics, with its concepts of matter, energy, and mind, might someday provide a framework within which such phenomena can be intelligently discussed.

The idea of the ancient theology is similar in many respects to the prophetic cycle in Islam. The Islamic list of prophets includes pre-Jewish ones (Seth, Noah), the Jews Abraham and Moses, and Jesus, before ending with Mohammed. As explained in the next chapter, Hermes Trismegistus and Agathodaimon gained admission as the prophets Idris and Seth. So Christianity, Judaism, and some forms of paganism were all accepted by the Muslims as inspired by divine revelation. In the West, Cardinal Nicholas of Cusa (1400/01–64) was virtually alone in returning the compliment. On his journey in the opposite direction to Gemistos's, going in 1437 as envoy to Byzantium, he received a revelation of the unity of religions. As a consequence, he faced the unavoidable fact that the Ottoman Sultan was conquering the Byzantine Empire by allowing that Islam and Christianity were not incompatible, and that Christian subjects could live under the secular rule of a Muslim.

In the Muslim world, the ancient theology had been formulated long before by the Persian theosopher Suhrawardi ("the Martyr," 1153–91).[11] He took the pagan teachings known to him—those of the real Zoroaster, Hermes Trismegistus, and Plato—and combined them with Shi'ite Islam.[12] At the center of Suhrawardi's theosophy is the same concept of a spiritual body that is developed by prayer and meditation. In this body, the adept can explore an inner

world of supreme variety and wonder. Suhrawardi calls it
Hūrqalyā. His French translator and interpreter, Henry
Corbin, uses the term *mundus imaginalis* (the Imaginal
World), urging his readers never to confuse it with the
"imaginary" world of fantasy and fiction.[13] *Hūrqalyā* is a
real world, only it does not have a material substratum. It
answers to the requirements of the scientific method,
namely that anyone with the right equipment will discover
its objective existence. However, unlike the radio telescope
or particle collider, which inform the scientist of invisible and almost unimaginable realities, the exploration of
Hūrqalyā requires the special tool of a highly refined astral
or spiritual body: something as rare and hard to obtain as
any piece of expensive hardware.

The Persian theosophers made it their business to
explore this imaginal world, which, being superior in the
cosmic hierarchy to the material world, has a formative and
controlling effect on the latter. As one reads in the encyclopedia of the Brethren of Purity, a tenth-century community of mystics in southeast Iraq, "it is the angels (whose
symbols are the planets) who keep order in the motion of
the heavens and who generate the minerals as well as plants
and animals."[14] For want of contemporary guidebooks,
Suhrawardi called on Zoroastrian scriptures such as the
liturgical *Avesta* and the cosmogonic *Bundahishn.* These
told stories of Zoroaster that only make sense when situ-
ated in *Hūrqalyā*: stories of his encounters with heavenly
beings, ascent to inaccessible mountaintops, and the bestowal
of his *Xvarnah* or radiant body.

The nearest analogue to this radiance on earth is fire. In
the Zoroastrian religion, still surviving among the Parsees of

India, all ritual centers around the sacred fire. As always, the symbols and rites of exoteric religion have an inner meaning that is first to be understood, then experienced by the esoteric adventurer. Likewise, the *Chaldean Oracles*, fragmentary as they are, are filled with fire imagery. Fire, as the subtlest of the four elements, is emblematic of the substances and energies out of which the God of the *Oracles* made the world.

The Juliani were "theurgists," i.e., performers of rituals for obtaining communication with the gods. Some theurgy is objective, commanding or inviting the gods to manifest themselves. They may then appear visibly (usually as light-forms), or speak through a medium, or be felt as a presence. Another branch of theurgy is subjective, in which the communication takes place internally, as in prayer or vision. The voyages of the Persian theosophers to *Hūrqalyā* were of this nature (substituting angels for gods). The *Chaldean Oracles* contain evidence for both kinds of invocation. In the tremendous final fragments, with their description of the visions that throng in upon the adept after frequent invocation, one is told: "When thou shalt behold that holy and formless Fire shining flashingly through the depths of the Universe: Hear thou the voice of Fire."[15] Thomas Taylor, the eighteenth-century Platonist and translator, believed that while many of the *Oracles* came from the Juliani, some of them, including the one just quoted, went back to the original Zoroaster. If he was correct, there is a continuity of theurgists running from ancient Persia through the Juliani, Suhrawardi, and Plethon, feeding the stream of European magic (Ficino, Agrippa), and continuing to this day.

CHAPTER

2

The Hermetic Tradition

he idea of a primordial wisdom leading directly from the Egyptian Hermes Trismegistus to the Greek Orpheus had more than a grain of truth in it. Even though the Egypt of classical times was far past its zenith, its temple traditions attracted aspirants of the caliber of Pythagoras and Plato, who made the journey to gain its initiations and incorporate them into their own philosophies. At the level of popular religion, the Egyptian cults entered the classical world in the fourth century B.C. with Alexander the Great's conquests. Alexander himself was pictured with the ram-horns of the Theban god Amon. To Rome went the goddess Isis, whose cult became one of the most splendid of the imperial era. In Alexandria and other Greek-speaking centers, a new god, Serapis, arose as a friendly rival to Zeus. Ibis-headed Thoth reappeared under the turban of Mercurius Trismegistus, Thrice-Greatest Hermes.

In polytheism, each god or goddess has a particular function. Each is an aspect of the unknowable One, and doubtless they all point to the same goal, but each appeals to a different psychospiritual type. Thoth, in Egyptian mythology, was the first giver of useful knowledge to mankind. A god who relates to mankind by giving knowledge is far different from a suffering savior god like Osiris or Jesus, or a loving mother goddess like Isis or the Virgin Mary, and will attract a different type of devotee. The way that leads through knowledge is, on the whole, an esoteric path, as opposed to the exoteric one of devotional religion. This knowledge, which is the goal of true philosophy, has a dual purpose. First, it teaches techniques and practices for overcoming human limitations, such as the trauma of death. Second, it studies the cosmic order and seeks to work within it. Wherever these two purposes meet, we have a form of Hermetism.

In Egyptian myth, Thoth is described variously as the spirit and intelligence of the Creator; god of learning and of healing; judge of celestial disputes and secretary of the gods; weigher of the souls of the dead. It was he who uttered the words that reunited the severed members of Osiris after the latter's murder by Set. Thoth invented numbers; he measured time and created the calendar. At his most abstract, he was a god of transitions: from chaos to cosmos, strife to friendship, death to rebirth, causes to effects. More concretely, he was seen by the people as a god of magic spells and astrology, folk medicine, and the lore of plants and minerals.

All of these qualities followed Thoth as the Alexandrian Greeks adopted him,[1] finding the nearest equivalent in their own pantheon as Hermes. The Greek god Hermes had also been a god of transitions: a marker of boundaries, guide of souls to Hades, messenger between Olympus and earth, patron of merchants and thieves. When his name was given to Thoth, with the epithet Trismegistus, he moved up the social scale, becoming a philosopher-king. Thus he recreated for the Hellenistic age the memory of those divine men, or incarnate gods, who are said to have been the first teachers and lawgivers of the human race. There are echoes of them in every land: in India as Rama, Krishna, and Manu; in Persia as Zoroaster; in China as Fo-Hi; in the Americas as Quetzalcoatl and Viracocha; in Greece as Dionysus and Orpheus, in Ireland as the Tuatha Dé Danann; and in Northern Europe as Odin.

Gradually Hermes Trismegistus acquired a body of scripture of his own, now known as the *Corpus Hermeticum*.[2] Generally dated to between the first and third centuries A.D., it is a collection of doctrinal and inspirational writings by several authors, playing variations around a few great themes: the absolute goodness of God, who is both One and All; the self-revelation of the Divine Mind in the cosmos; the universe as a emanation of living beings in hierarchical order; the unique constitution of the human being as microcosm; the way to regeneration and the direct knowledge of God. The Hermetic scriptures restated these themes for the benefit of cosmopolitan Greek-speakers living under the Roman Empire.

Just as Thoth had a popular side, so Hermes became a master of the occult sciences, a revealer of astrological medicine and of the sympathetic magic by which one draws down influences from the heavens and fixes them in talismans. An example occurs in the Latin Hermetic text *Asclepius*, in the description of how the Egyptians infused gods into statues: an idea that both fascinated and scared Christian writers.[3] Last but not least, Hermes's natural philosophy and secret knowledge joined to make him the father of alchemy, the Egyptian art of transmutation. It is no chance that alchemy accords such a vital role to Mercury, both as the most mysterious of the known metals and as a symbol of the elusive faculty of the soul that mediates between matter and spirit. The transmutation in question could be understood chemically, as turning base metals into gold, but also in terms of inner transformations within the human being (see chapter 13).

Another mythic image for the latter process occurs in the first treatise of the *Corpus Hermeticum*, "Poimandres."[4] It is the description of the ascent of the soul after death, and the surrendering of its energies to the successive spheres of the seven planets. (The cosmos is assumed to be geocentric, with the earth at the center surrounded, like the layers of an onion, by the spheres of the moon, planets, sun, and stars.) When the soul has given up all its downward tendencies, it can soar up through the eighth sphere (the fixed stars) and join the company of the Blessed. This is a cosmic version of the ordeal described in the Egyptian *Book of the Dead* (or *The Book of Coming Forth by Day*), where the soul must traverse the several halls of the Otherworld and be weighed against a feather, before it can enter the paradise of Osiris.[5]

The philosophic side of Hermetism is based on the doctrine of correspondences. In the Hermetic ascent, each planet corresponds to a certain power of the soul: Mercury to the intelligence, Venus to desire, Mars to anger, etc. The human being is thus a microcosm, containing in little the same energies as the macrocosm. If we picture earth at the center of the universe, the soul has acquired these energies on its downward (or inward) journey from the celestial regions through the planetary spheres. It emerges into earth life via the womb, full of potentials and tendencies that are delineated by its natal horoscope. Through life it works with these potentials, hopefully refining them so that they emerge as virtues. If this is accomplished, the soul when it leaves the body at death is light and unencumbered, and well able to rise upward (or outward) to the place of its origin. If instead the energies have coagulated in vices, then the upward journey will be difficult and the soul may even remain trapped in the earth's atmosphere, a torment to itself and a bane to its fellows.

After the Roman Empire, Hermetism, or the religious philosophy that gave rise to the *Corpus Hermeticum,* expanded to include alchemy and the occult sciences (divination, astrology, magic, etc.). All three Abrahamic religions (Judaism, Christianity, Islam) found a place for it, though sometimes a grudging one. It entered Islam thanks to the Sabaeans of Harran, the center of an ancient copper industry now in Turkey near the Syrian border. The Sabaeans, who receive favorable mention in the Qur'an, blended star worship with Neopythagoreanism, Neoplatonism, and practical alchemy.[6] Their patron divinities were Hermes and Agathodaimon, who were made respectable as the Muslim prophets Idris (= the Enoch of the Bible) and Adam's son Seth. For a century or more Harran was also the home of a school of translators who specialized in Greek mathematics and astronomy, thus transmitting much of the Pythagorean tradition to the Muslim world. Their work was taken over in the tenth century by the Brethren of Purity of Basra (Iraq), who compiled an encyclopedia of all the arts and sciences, including theurgy and magic. This was studied by the Druses, by the sect of the Assassins, and by most Sufi schools, in which it is still read today. In this way, Hermetism has passed into the very heart of Islamic esotericism.

In Judaism, the Hermetic influences emerged in the Kabbalah. The short and fundamental Kabbalistic text *Sepher Yetzirah*[7] (the "Book of Creation," third century A.D.?) expounds a cosmology based on the doctrine of correspondences, notably the sevenfold one of the planets, days of the week, openings in the head and body, etc., and the twelvefold one of the zodiac, directions of space, months, organs of the body, etc. It describes a cosmos not torn between good and evil, but held in polarity by positive and negative energies. The method of salvation is through becoming aware of oneself as a microcosm, seating the "King on his Throne" (the divine presence) in the center of life. Again we have a doctrine that is affirmative of nature and the body, and dedicated to the realization of the macrocosm in the microcosm. The esoteric idea of Israel is also a Hermetic one: it is that the Jews are called upon to bear witness to the divine order on earth. Just as in Hermetism the earth, including the human body, is replete with celestial influences, so the Jewish way of life is designed to ensure that every action carries a spiritual significance.

In the West, the only Hermetic treatise known through the Middle Ages was the *Asclepius,* which was viewed with some mistrust as a magical text. Only in 1460 did the greater part of the *Corpus Hermeticum* arrive in Florence;

one of Cosimo de' Medici's scouts had discovered a manu-script in Macedonia. Three years later, Marsilio Ficino pre-sented his translation to the aged Cosimo, and for the next century and a half the Hermetic writings had a marked effect on the intellectual world. The idea that God had spoken not only to the Jews but to the pagans led, in select circles, to the renewal of a universal religious sense, such as had last existed under the Roman Empire. In the Renais-sance era, the Hermetic philosophy served as neutral ground for Protestants and Catholics alike. Alchemy and the other occult sciences to which it provided the intellectual under-pinning flourished as never before.

Because it is essentially a cosmological and practical teaching, rather than a theology, Hermetism can coexist with any religion. It offers an analysis of the human condi-tion within the cosmos, and a variety of methods for mak-ing the best use of this condition. Its historical record is innocent of intolerance and bloodshed, its way of life one of science, contemplation, and self-refinement. For these reasons, the Hermetic territory is an ideal meeting place for Christians, Jews, Muslims, and those of other religions or none. John Michell writes of how the Hermetic science of sacred geometry, which he demonstrates as underlying the city of Jerusalem, might potentially unite "Jews to the east, Muslims to the south, Christians to the west and, in the direction of the north pole, followers of that ancient religious system that preceded the others."[8]

Freemasonry, which arose in its present form in the seventeenth and eighteenth centuries, was the most last-ing creation of the Hermetic tradition in the West, carrying it through the era of skepticism and scientism. Masonic symbolism is thoroughly Hermetic, even when it is not obviously Egyptian. The image of the Great Architect of the Universe, forming humans as rough stones to be worked into perfect blocks for the cosmic Temple, goes back to Plato's Demiurge: the creator of the physical cosmos on mathematical principles, as described in Plato's dialogue *Timaeus*. The stages of Masonic initiation are like the steps on the Hermetic ascent, complete with their planetary symbolism. And the rule of avoiding religious discussion in the lodge eliminates one of the chief obstacles to human brotherhood: sectarian discord.

However, if we try to penetrate this deeper wisdom with the help of modern Hermetic schools, we meet a more esoteric and perhaps disturbing doctrine. According to these schools, while the essence of each human is immortal, it is also impersonal. The personality does not survive, at least not long after bodily death, and consequently there is nothing left of most people's souls once they have been filtered through the planetary spheres.[9] The vast majority will be extinguished as personalities soon after death, while their essence may be recycled as entirely different entities. To put it plainly, there is no guarantee of personal immortality, whatever comforting doctrines may say to the contrary. The ambition of the Hermetic adept is to survive this general dissolution, and if he should incarnate again, to do so only through deliberate choice, not through bondage to a natural process like everyone else. In order to pass beyond the boundaries of the cosmos (symbolized by the starry sphere) and enter consciously into another mode of existence, the adept must have forged, during life, a "radiant body" as vehicle for his individuality.[10] This is obviously similar to the process described in the *Chaldean Oracles* and discussed in the previous chapter.

But it would be a great mistake to assume that only the adept's life is worthwhile, because only he or she achieves personal immortality. In a sense, the adept's goal of preserving individuality is against nature, and because, like all science, it is amoral, it may preserve evil personalities as well as good ones. As one of the few experts in this field writes: "The *permanent* preservation of a personal identity beyond death is a very rare achievement, accomplished only by those who wrest her secrets from Nature, and control their own super-material development. . . . [It is] accomplished only by adepts and sorcerers—the one class having acquired the supreme secret knowledge by holy methods, and with benevolent motives, the other having acquired it by unholy methods, and for base motives."[11]

Hermetism is not limited to the aim of personal immortality in this sense. Unlike the world-rejecting philosophies, it accepts and joyfully embraces the entire process of incarnation and excarnation. The physical world, because it is infused with celestial influences, is a place of beauty and wonder. Nature is a book from which the wisdom of the divine Mind can be read. Thoth, we recall, was concerned with *useful* knowledge: arts and sciences that improve the quality of life, such as music and mathematics and writing. Alchemy itself obviously began with the technology of metals. Wherever mere animal existence is enhanced by the arts or sciences, and people become aware of the divine Mind through the works of Nature, the gifts of Thoth are bearing fruit.

CHAPTER

3

The Orphic Mysteries

he distant figure of Hermes Trismegistus seems
superhuman, without faults and equally without character, and the same goes for Zoroaster,
at least until the late nineteenth century, when Nietzsche
humanized and humorized him in *Also Sprach Zarathustra*.
Imagining Orpheus is a different matter. Most people can
recall two things about him: that he was a musician, and
that he went down to the Underworld to fetch his wife
Eurydice. His story is the archetypal myth of the power
of music. With the lyre that was a gift from Apollo,
Orpheus could move everything in creation, from stones,
trees, and beasts, through humans, to daimonic and even
divine beings (whom we might call angels and gods).
Armed only with his songs, he charmed the denizens of
Hades and persuaded Pluto and Persephone to let him take
Eurydice back.

Orpheus was a prince of Thrace, the land to the north of Greece. His mother was Calliope, the Muse of epic poetry. Some say that his father was Apollo, and certainly Orpheus stands under the patronage of that god. Apollo also had northern connections, either coming from Hyperborea (the land beyond the North Wind), or else visiting that far northern land after his birth on the island of Delos. Where was this Hyperborea? As it was said to contain a circular temple to the sun, some have identified it with Britain, and its temple with Stonehenge, a monument far older than any in Greece.

Stonehenge, and the people who constructed it, were Apollonian in the sense of being dedicated to the sun, to astronomy, mathematics, and music. A number of modern researchers have penetrated beyond the limitations of academic prehistory to reveal, through intuition, the bases of this ancient science. John Michell, the pioneer in this regard, has reconstructed the diagrams and dimensions that seem to lie at the basis of megalithic design.[1] Jean Richer has shown that there is an imaginary zodiac whose twelvefold symbolism links mythology with the geography of the Aegean area.[2] Paul Broadhurst and Hamish Miller have traced a plethora of Apollonian sites in geometrical alignment, all the way from Ireland to Palestine.[3] Michell, in addition, has traced the myth of "perpetual choirs" maintained at ancient sanctuaries for the purpose of what he calls "enchanting the landscape."[4] If one is attentive to such findings, it is clear that there was a high and orderly civilization well established by the third millennium B.C., of which the archaeologists know almost nothing.

This enchantment of the landscape is exactly what Orpheus is reputed to have done with his music, casting a benign spell over nature and bringing peace among men. As part of his mission, he reformed the cult of Dionysus (Bacchus) and tried to persuade its followers to give up their blood sacrifices. In place of the Dionysian orgies, Orpheus founded the first Mysteries of Greece. The purpose of these, as far as we can tell, was to transmit some kind of direct knowledge that was helpful in facing the prospect of death.

Orpheus's journey to the Underworld to fetch Eurydice should be understood in the context of the Mysteries.[5] In the earliest versions of the myth, he did succeed in restoring her to life. Only later was the episode embroidered by the poets[6] so that it ended tragically, as Orpheus at the last moment disobeyed the ban on looking at his wife before he reached the surface of the earth, and lost her again forever. Orpheus was originally a psychopomp (leader of souls) who had the power to rescue souls from the gray, dreamlike condition that was believed in archaic times to be the inevitable fate of the dead. Initiates of the Mysteries received the assurance that this would not be their fate, and that like Eurydice they would be saved from Pluto's dismal realm. This was the first time that the immortality of the soul was taught on Greek soil, beginning a tradition that Pythagoras, Socrates, and Plato would each enhance in his own way (see chapters 4 and 5).

Most of what we know of Orphism derives from much later even than these philosophers. Under the Roman Empire, around the time of early Christianity, there was a strong resurgence of Orphism as a mystery religion. The *Orphic Hymns*, a set of magical incantations addressed to the various gods and daimons, date from this revival.[7] Far from discarding the worship of Dionysus, Orphism now made him the very core of its doctrine. One of the myths of Dionysus tells that as an infant he was captured by the Titans (the rivals of the gods), who dismembered and ate him. Fortunately Zeus was able to save his son's heart. He swallowed it himself, and in due time gave Dionysus second birth. The Titans were vanquished, and out of their remains came human beings. Consequently, every human body contains a tiny fragment of Dionysus.

It is easy to recognize in this myth the doctrine, familiar now but by no means common then, that each person is not just a compound of body and soul, but also possesses a spark of absolute divinity. Religions that hold this doctrine are aimed at retrieving, reviving, and eventually realizing that spark, either in life or after death. To realize it—to "make it real"—is to become oneself a god, and henceforth immortal. That is the ultimate promise of the Mysteries. For the uninitiated, there is only the prospect of Hades, a place not of torment except for the very wicked, but not of pleasure, either, even for the best of men. Eventually the soul there withers and dies, releasing the divine spark to reincarnate in another body and soul.

This touches once again on the matter of conditional immortality (see chapter 2), which is a constant concern of esoteric teaching and practice. The distinction is implicit as early as Homer's *Odyssey,* though the relevant passage is probably an interpolation from classical times. When Odysseus sees the heroes in Hades, even the greatest of them is stuck there without hope of ascent, redemption, or rebirth. A single exception is made for Hercules. Odysseus, it is said, saw only his image in Hades, while Hercules "himself" is among the eternal gods.[8]

Hercules here represents the initiate, who is supposedly freed from this wheel of birth and death and is able to proceed to a more glorious destiny among the gods. As a reminder, the Orphic initiates were not buried with pots of food and furniture, but cremated and buried with gold leaves inscribed in Greek.[9] These carry prayers and instructions about what they should say and do upon awakening after death. They must avoid at all costs drinking from the Lake of Lethe (forgetfulness), but instead turn to the right, to the Lake of Mnemosyne (memory), and address its guardians in these beautiful words: "I am the child of earth and of starry Heaven. This you yourselves also know. I am dry with thirst and am perishing. Come, give me at once cold water flowing forth from the Lake of Memory." Or, on meeting the rulers of Hades, they should say: "I come pure from the pure, Queen of the Underworld, Eucles, Eubouleus, and all other gods! For I too claim to be of your race."

By the Roman period, as we read in Ovid's version of his story,[10] the figure of Orpheus had become a tragic one. Not only did he lose Eurydice for the second time, but he himself suffered a cruel death. It is said that he returned to his native Thrace to try to reform the inhabitants, but fell afoul of the Maenads, women followers of the unregenerate rites of Dionysus. Screaming to silence his magical songs, they tore him limb from limb. But his head floated to the sea and lodged in a rock on the isle of Lesbos, where it continued to sing. He himself was taken up by his father Apollo, and his lyre was raised to the stars as the constellation Lyra.

With this version of his myth, Orpheus took his place among the other suffering saviors whose cults were popular in cosmopolitan Rome: Dionysus, Attis, Adonis, Hercules, Osiris, and Jesus of Nazareth.[11] These divine beings offered a personal relationship with their worshipers that many people found more satisfying than the distant Olympian gods. The implication was that as the gods had suffered, died, and returned to their native heaven, so would their followers.

Some of the early Christians regarded Orpheus as a kind of pagan saint, even confusing his image with that of Jesus. Both saviors were demigods of royal descent who sought to refashion an existing religion in the interests of humanitarianism. Both descended into Hades to rescue loved ones from eternal death. (Jesus' descent into Hades to deliver the souls of the Old Testament fathers is not biblical, but has been standard doctrine since the second century).[12] Their religions taught the potential immortality of the soul, depending on one's actions in life. Both suffered tragic deaths as sacrifices to the religions they had tried to reform: Orpheus, as the dismembered victim of the Dionysian orgy; Jesus, in the image of the Lamb slain for the Passover supper. Their relations with their parent religions were highly ambiguous. Jesus, while acknowledging the Jewish god Yahweh as his heavenly father, treated the Mosaic Law with disdain, and supposedly died on the cross to appease his father's anger with humanity. Orpheus was killed by the sectaries of Dionysus, imitating the latter's death at the hands of the Titans.

The importance placed on the next life encouraged Orphics and Christians alike to defer their pleasures in this one. Both groups sought to live a life of chastity and abstinence (the Orphics were vegetarians) that was incongruous with the society around them. It was also cause for surprise that both practiced friendship to strangers, not merely to people of their own race and creed, as the Greeks and Jews tended to do. But this was a natural conclusion from the principle that each person was in essence divine. Consequently Orphism was the first religion in Europe, and perhaps the first anywhere, to preach what we think of as "Christian" virtues, to promise an afterlife whose quality depended on their practice, and to institute mysteries as a foretaste of the soul's future destiny.

The Orphics had been the first philosophers of Greece and the spiritual ancestors of the Pythagorean and Platonic schools, renowned for asceticism and for belief in the immortality of the soul. Now, in the Orphic revival, they stamped their principles on the new religion. Through numerical coding of key words and phrases in the Greek (New) Testament, Christianity was linked with the Pythagorean tradition, in which music and number were the first principles of the universe.[13] But this knowledge was not for general consumption. In two respects, Orphism was the first known esoteric religion. First, it imposed the seal of the Mysteries, so that the teachings given in initiation were not revealed to outsiders. Second, it gave a profounder, symbolic interpretation to existing myths such as the Theogony (the genealogy of the Greco-Roman gods). Mysteries and the knowledge of hidden meanings in the scriptures have since been two of the chief marks of esotericism.

The Orphic impulse survives to this day, not in religion so much as in the arts, of which Apollo is the traditional

patron and the Muses the inspirers. These "arts" were originally disciplines that were closer in some ways to what we
call sciences: they included history and astronomy, along
with dance, music, poetry, and drama.[14] Their effects were
calculated, even in the literal sense of being governed by
mathematics. This is obvious in the cases of astronomy and
music. But poetry, too, is speech controlled by rhythmic
number; dance is rhythmic and geometrical movement;
drama and history control the unruly memories and rumors
of earthly and divine events and turn them into moral and
philosophical lessons. Whatever the status of the arts today,
the Muses were originally not in the business of entertain-
ing people but of civilizing them, using deliberate and
highly developed techniques based, for the most part, on
number. This brings us back to the elaborate mathematics
of Stonehenge and other prehistoric monuments, and to
John Michell's vision of a civilization held in a state of grace
by the tireless chanting of a mantic song, its music ruled by
number and proportion.[15]

Orpheus, singing to Apollo's lyre, is said to have had the
power to move every kind of body and soul. He could force
apart the Clashing Rocks so that the ship of the Argonauts
could pass safely between them; he succeeded in touching
the hearts of the chthonic gods. Stones that have been
"moved" and set in geometrical order are the substance both
of Stonehenge and of the Greek temples, monuments that
even in their ruin command awed respect and convey a
sense of sublime harmony. Music, too, though it may
consist of nothing more than air vibrating according to
mathematical laws, has always had an unaccountable power
to touch the heart and exalt the spirit. In a well-ordered

civilization, the two arts of architecture and music work in consort: the first, to provide harmonious surroundings for the body and to delight the eye; the second to delight the ear and to bring about harmony in the soul. Recent researches by Paul Devereux, Robert Jahn, and others, suggest that this link of stone buildings with music goes back to the Stone Age.[16]

The Orphic and Apollonian ideal manifests in all those works of art that we call "classic." They are not exclusive to Greece by any means. In ancient China, for example, a hieratic music, along with religious ceremonies, was recognized as the best means of procuring peace in the empire and the good government of its citizens.[17] Mexico also has a version of Apollonian classicism in the architecture of the Mayas and their predecessors, which, like the European stone circles, was geometrically planned and cosmically oriented.[18] The West has had classic phases in all the arts whenever the peak of a certain style is reached, and with it an image of harmonious diversity as reassuring as the regular passage of the sun through the seasons.

In Western music, the seven strings of Apollo's lyre are sounded as the diatonic scale (the white notes of the piano). Their most "classic" manifestation is not in Bach or Mozart but in plainsong, which served the Christian Church for fifteen hundred years or more before it was pushed aside by more glamorous types of music, then discarded altogether. The calming, healing, and uplifting power of unaccompanied chant is intuitively felt by the soul, just as it was in the time of Orpheus. The fact that it was employed for a time in Christian worship and given Latin words is a secondary matter.

Do music and the arts directly affect the quality of a civilization? No one can say for certain whether this Orphic premise is correct, because it has not been put into practice in modern times. Totalitarian governments have made a mockery of the idea. The Nazis banned atonal music because it was incomprehensible to their cultural pundits, and jazz because it was African-American in origin. The Russian Communists banned atonal music for the same reason, and rock 'n' roll because it was associated with protest and Western influence. These were hardly the proper motives for controlling a people's music. But the rulers in question were not philosopher-kings,[19] who alone might be expected to have their subjects' spiritual interests at heart, and to have the knowledge of how to further them.

Even if depravity in the arts is not the cause of moral decay, it unfortunately mirrors many people's spiritual state. The art critic Suzi Gablik, once a prominent mouthpiece for modernism, writes of how she emerged into this realization after an "acute crisis of credibility about the core truths of modernity—secularism, individualism, bureaucracy, and pluralism—by which the numinous, the mythic, and the sacramental have been, in our society, reduced to rags."[20] When the arts are profane and purposeless, and dwell on ugliness and vice, one can be sure that the collective soul is not in good health. If the Orphics are right, this is as serious a matter as the malnutrition of our nation's poor. The outlook is bleak for those souls nourished only by the junk food and poisonous additives of popular culture. How will it be for them to enter the soul's domain with no songs to sing, no poetry to charm Pluto and Persephone?

The Orphic, and the Christian, solution is not to force people but to gently persuade them toward a better way. One can see this in the actions of the founders, as they tried to reform the Dionysian and Mosaic traditions. One can also see it in America's founders, who absorbed Orphic principles through Freemasonry, and deliberately chose freedom, not rigor, as the school for their citizens.[21] With an optimism that, on good days, we may still share, they allowed each person to regulate his or her own religious, aesthetic, and private life. In chapter 5, when we come to Plato's prescriptions, we will consider the contrary policy.

CHAPTER

4

Pythagoras and His School

As we enter the historical period, that which is mythical and mysterious in Orpheus moves closer to mundane reality. We may doubt that Pythagoras had a golden thigh and could hear the music of the spheres.[1] But unlike Hermes Trismegistus, Zoroaster, and Orpheus, his existence is beyond question. He was born early in the sixth century B.C. on the Aegean island of Samos, spent years in Egypt and Chaldea, and passed his later life in Crotona on the coast of southern Italy. Here he had a family, founded a school of philosophy, and died at an advanced age.

Orpheus's lyre, which charmed everything from stones to gods, became in Pythagoras's hands a scientific instrument, used to operate on human emotions. Whereas Orpheus, if he ever existed, performed in a mantic and inspired state, Pythagoras knew exactly which musical mode had which psychological effect. He could adjust the dose to the patient's needs, as in the anecdote of the enraged youth who calmed down when Pythagoras told the musician to change the mode in which he was playing. For his own pupils, he prescribed music that would help them in their ascetic life and studies.

Whereas Orpheus was a poet, Pythagoras was an intellectual and an experimenter. He did not just use music, but was interested in how it worked and set up experiments to discover this. Like later scientists, he expressed his discoveries in mathematical formulae, such as the geometrical theorem still known by his name,[2] and the musical formula 12:9:8:6, which defines the primary consonances.[3] At least, his disciples assumed that they were his own discoveries. It is much more likely that he refined them from what he had learned during his long periods of residence abroad, from the wise men of Memphis and Babylon. Such things had been known in those civilizations for hundreds of years; they were new only to the Greeks.[4]

The genius of Pythagoras was to make a synthesis of scientific knowledge learned abroad with the local Orphic mystery religion, and on this combined basis to found the first philosophical school in Europe. Philosophy, literally "the love of wisdom," is a term that includes both heart and head, implying that one alone is not sufficient. For the mystery religions, love was enough. In the Orphic cult it took the form of friendliness towards all creation; the worship of the gods, especially Apollo; and the aspiration that, after death, one might escape the bondage of earth and become united with the gods in their own realm. All of this was carried over into the Pythagorean community. They were vegetarians because they refused to harm animate creatures. They practiced private and public philanthropy, getting involved in politics in the interests of the wider community. They were devotees of Apollo, and believed in an afterlife whose condition depended on one's present conduct.

What made the Pythagoreans a school and not just a religious community was that they also cultivated their intellects. They listened to lectures with a patience and a passivity that astonishes us—neophytes had to listen to Pythagoras from behind a curtain and had to keep silent for five years before they could even ask a question. They learned mathematics, astronomy, and the science of the monochord. This was a kind of wisdom that could only be cultivated by those who were in love with it; anyone who did not would be unbearably bored. As a result, the Pythagoreans did not just undergo spiritual experiences: they understood them, passing the distillations of the heart through the sieve of the intellect.

There had been esoteric schools before the time of Pythagoras, both in Egypt and in the megalithic cultures some thousands of years previously. The presence of sophisticated geometry and arithmetic in the stone circles of Britain[5] and the golden artifacts of mainland Europe[6] proves as much. But around the middle of the second millennium B.C., a dark age seems to have intervened, perhaps due to some geological or cosmic cataclysm, putting an end to the "prehistoric" era and its institutions.[7] The revival of culture in the Greek and Italian regions necessitated new forms and institutions. Pythagoras's school was one of the first of these.

Only a miniscule part of the population qualified as "philosophers" in the Pythagorean sense. This is as true today as it was in the sixth century B.C. For the benefit of these few, Pythagoras formed a school and imposed on his pupils the obligation of silence, thus founding the first secret and esoteric society in European history. Secrecy is out of favor in our times, because of the official fiction that everyone is equal, hence entitled to the same information. Therefore one has to explain the traditional reserve of such schools. From the point of view of a member of an esoteric school, learning is a progressive and evolutionary matter, and if one talks about it prematurely one will almost certainly give a faulty and distorted impression of it. In esoteric work one goes through many periods of illusion and disillusion, which, if regularly aired about, would give a terrible impression to outsiders and possibly arouse their hostility. Besides, there is quasi-alchemical advantage to keeping the vessel sealed, and not letting anything out of it, or into it, while the Work is in progress.

From the point of view of those outside the school, it is preferable to know nothing than to receive faulty and distorted versions of its teachings from talkative neophytes. Such misinformation is bad for its receivers, because without going the whole course they will get the wrong ideas into their heads about extremely important matters. Outsiders are much better off following an exoteric religion than dabbling in things they have no talent for.

This attitude is elitist, or better said, hierarchical, and entirely consistent with the doctrine of reincarnation (the return of souls into other bodies) that was one of the pillars of Pythagorean metaphysics.[8] Such an attitude does not regard a human life as a once-for-all matter, but as it were a single bead of a necklace. If on the contrary everyone has only one life, it is indeed unfair that some should have come into it with silver spoons in their mouths, others with disadvantages of body, mind, and circumstances. Strange and complicated motives have to be attributed to a god or gods to excuse such a state of affairs. But reincarnation supplies its believers both with a cause of one's present state, to be sought in preceding lives, and with hope for earning happier rebirths in the future. Every person is a soul in temporary embodiment, captive in the body he or she has deserved.

It is not my business either to defend or to attack this theory, but only to clarify it. Nor will I attempt to reconcile it with the doctrine mentioned in the preceding chapters, namely that the survival of the individual soul is a rare and hard-won phenomenon. Of all the subjects on which esotericists fail to agree, that of the soul's destiny—whether or not it is reincarnated on earth—is the thorniest. Perhaps there is not single, universal answer, because different souls may follow different destinies.[9]

Pythagoras, following Orpheus, taught the inevitability of reembodiment, but also its undesirability. The Orphic symbol of the cosmic wheel to which we are bound holds out the hope of somehow getting off the wheel and never again having to return to a body: hence the expression *soma sema*, meaning that the *soma*, Greek for "body," is a *sema*, meaning "tomb," for the soul. This is the whole *raison d'être* of the mystery religions. People go round and round on the wheel, from birth to birth, until they are ready for the initiation that enables them to take aim, at least, for states beyond the human one.[10] But it is futile for them to try this flight before they have developed the wings of initiation. This is one meaning of the myth of Daedalus and Icarus.

The Pythagorean school can be usefully compared with another institution contemporary with it, the Eleusinian Mysteries.[11] Far from requiring years of preparation and a rigidly ascetic life, the initiations of Eleusis were available to any Greek-speaking person who was not a murderer, including women and probably even slaves.[12] A certain ritual series of acts had to be performed, relating to the myth of Demeter and Persephone. They began with the procession from Athens and climaxed in the great hypostyle hall of Eleusis. We still do not know exactly what happened there, but something was seen or witnessed that had an enduring effect. Afterwards, the initiates felt a new confidence, especially regarding the afterlife.

The Eleusinian Mysteries resemble a much later institution: the *hajj*, the pilgrimage to Mecca that all Muslims are enjoined, if possible, to make once in their lives. There are many parallels with Islamic practices, such as the abstention from food during daylight (for Muslims, in the month of Ramadan), animal sacrifice, the ritual reenactment of the sufferings of Demeter and Hagar, respectively, the procession, and the sense of oneness with a great crowd in a most sacred place. Every element contributes to the emotional force of the event, making it a life-changing experience that fortifies one's faith.

While the Eleusinian Mysteries were in a sense esoteric, for they bound their initiates to secrecy, the experience they afforded did not require the participation of the rational mind. In contrast, the esoteric schools from Pythagoras's onwards require the active cultivation of the intellect. Their goal is not a spiritual roller-coaster ride but a lifetime of steady spiritual and intellectual work, in which every experiential advance is accompanied by understanding.

Pythagoras's curriculum used the sciences of number—mathematics, music, and probably astronomy—to hone the student's intelligence to a fine edge. This kind of study cannot have been common in the sixth century B.C. We ultimately have Pythagoras to thank that it is taken for granted nowadays.[13] Most people learn much more mathematics in school than they will ever put to practical use, because it is believed that it trains the mind in a way useful for any discipline. Music, when studied both as a science, and an art,[14] provides the missing link between the head and the heart. Astronomy, which in past times always included astrology, links the calculated movements of the heavenly bodies with human character, behavior, and destiny, and connects with archaic theories of the afterlife. We have already seen something of this in the Hermetic doctrine of the ascent through the planetary spheres. The Pythagorean curriculum, in short, was intended to develop conscious and critical participation in the drama of life and death.

CHAPTER

5

Plato's Cave

The traditional lists of illuminated philosophers all leap over the century that separates
Pythagoras (sixth century B.C.) from Plato
(428–347 B.C.). Such improbable gaps apart,[1] the very
thread that once seemed to lead so tidily from one sage to
another is now tangled and knotted, for the writings once
ascribed to Zoroaster, Hermes, and Orpheus are themselves
Platonic: we know that they date from well after Plato's time
and reflect his influence. The question remains of how far
his own philosophy derived from more ancient sources. In
any case, his vision of a cosmos ordered in hierarchies and
bonded by love is, one hopes, close to the reality of things.
As we shall see, it provides both a metaphysical framework
for philosophy and guidelines for personal and political life.

Platonic metaphysics takes as its premise the existence
of a "world of Forms" that is the matrix from which the

material world arises. These Forms, far from being imaginary, are more real than what most people mistake for reality. We might call them archetypes: such things as Unity, Justice, Goodness, and Beauty, which are dimly reflected in what we know of these qualities.[2]

As the Platonic tradition developed, the Forms came to be identified with the gods and goddesses of pagan religion.[3] To the Neoplatonists, the personal beings that people worship are actually the Forms to which they feel a natural kinship.[4] Between these and the realm of matter stretches a chain of intermediate beings such as demigods and daimons, who also participate in their parent Forms and have a role in the governance of the world.[5] The entire cosmos is a hierarchy, suspended in pyramidal fashion from the One and its archetypal emanations.

How do we know this? Another Platonic principle is that like is known by like.[6] To know matter, one must have a physical body. To know immaterial things, one must have a soul. To know the Forms, one must have a higher intellect that is akin to them. Thus the individual is a microcosm of the whole.

But, the Platonists continue, in most of us these organs of knowledge are not fully developed. Most of what we know comes through the senses and is distorted by our opinions, so that we have only a vague notion of what it is. Higher and more accurate knowledge begins with the rational mind, and continues to the point of direct perception of the Forms through the impersonal intellect. Someone who sets out on this journey of self-development is a philosopher, a "wisdom-lover."

Plato's Myth of the Cave describes what happens to people who succeed in developing these higher degrees of perception.[7] Human beings are likened to prisoners in a cave, forced to sit and look at a wall. Behind them are the operators of the cave system, who use firelight and cutouts to project a shadow play on this wall, which the prisoners watch with absorbed interest, since it is all they know. It is just like a cinema. But once in a while, a prisoner manages to look around, and he sees to his surprise that the shadow play is not real, but created by the operators. He may even sneak out past them and discover the stairs that lead to the world outside, where he is thrilled to find himself in a world infinitely more wonderful than what he has known. Here he encounters the originals of the shadow play: real people, trees, mountains, stars, etc., in all their glorious form and color. The philosopher, for that is what he now is, is moved by compassion for his old friends still chained in the cave, and burns to dispel their illusions. He returns to the cave to tell them of his discovery. But far from welcoming him, jumping up, and escaping to the real world, they meet his report with disbelief, mockery, and hatred. They cannot bear it that someone pretends to know better than they.

Thus Plato's teacher Socrates found, when an Athenian jury condemned him to death by hemlock poisoning in 399 B.C.; so did the philosopher Hypatia, when St. Cyril, bishop of Alexandria, incited a mob to dismember her in 415 A.D. These martyrdoms mark the dawn and the long twilight of the original Platonic tradition. When Plato's Academy was closed by the emperor Justinian in 529 A.D., it had lasted longer than any known educational institution up to that time.

The last philosophers of the Athenian Academy found refuge at the court of Persia.[8] From then on, the Platonic tradition led a largely underground existence. Although in its original form Platonism is incompatible with any of the three Abrahamic religions,[9] clever compromisers succeeded in adapting elements of it to each one, leaving its traces in Kabbalah, Christian theosophy, and Sufism.

Socrates had introduced to Plato and other young Athenians the subversive notion of questioning accepted beliefs and opinions. He used rational inquiry not so much to reach truth—that would be too much to ask—as to dispel illusion.[10] He taught his students, and forced his opponents, to admit their ignorance, as the necessary prelude to acquiring knowledge. This is the result of the famous "Socratic method."[11] But when Plato wants to make a positive statement out of his own convictions, he has Socrates use not dialectic but myth.[12] A myth is a tale that embodies higher truth, using symbols to kindle the imagination and stir the memory. All learning, for Socrates and Plato, is simply remembrance of what our souls once knew, but have forgotten.[13] We all came here from outside the cave.

A practical philosophy follows inevitably from this system. Its principle must be the separation of the soul from the material world and its reinstatement in its own domain. But no one would embark on this difficult and frustrating journey unless driven to it by overwhelming desire. The erotic element is an essential part of Platonic education; as the lover is drawn to the beloved, so the soul is drawn to the Forms of the Beautiful and the Good.[14] Carnal lust is the first step on the ladder of ascent through a cosmos suffused with desire in its every part. Every being in it, from the One downwards, emanates the next state of being, loves it as its own child, and is loved in return.[15] Platonists forget this at their peril, for hierarchy without Eros turns to tyranny, whether in the person, the family, or the state.

So we come to the vexed question of Platonic politics. Plato and Socrates receive a bad press these days because of their antidemocratic views.[16] At least we can understand why they could not think otherwise. Their ultimate reality consisted in the One and its emanated Forms (or gods), which give existence and shape to all else in the long descending chain of being. Human society, they thought, should mirror this. There must be a One—the monarch—and there must be Forms—the laws and their executors. But if the political hierarchy is to work, the monarch must emulate the wisdom of the model, society must be as orderly as the stars in their courses, and the levels of society must be joined through love. Has this ever happened?

Clearly not. One reason is that the necessary prescription has never yet been followed: that kings must be philosophers, and philosophers, in consequence, must become kings. Plato tried to groom Dionysius, future king of Syracuse in Sicily, for such a role, and failed when the young man escaped his moral control. The Roman Empire was more fortunate with its philosopher-emperors Hadrian, Marcus Aurelius, and Julian in the second and fourth centuries A.D. But an empire is far too large an entity for Platonic reform; the proper scale is that of the city-state. In fifteenth-century Florence, Cosimo de' Medici and his family graduated from bankers to philosophers under the tutelage of Gemistos Plethon and Marsilio Ficino, with magnificent results for the fine arts but little advantage to the populace. In eighteenth-century Weimar, where Johann Wolfgang von Goethe became the advisor and friend of

Duke Carl August (who ruled from 1775 to 1828), one can truly say that a philosopher was running if not ruling the state. This and other enlightened absolutisms of the Age of Enlightenment came as close to the Platonic ideal as any so far. But it was not very close.

The prospects are even more distant today. Ever since the Middle Ages, Western philosophy has had an Aristotelian bias, preferring to assert that knowledge derives from the ordinary sense-perception common to all people: a metaphysical position that disallows any claim of superior knowledge. Philosophy itself has earned itself a bad name since it degenerated from "wisdom-loving" into competing schools of thought, and finally into a series of fashionable intellectual poses. As for the fruits of higher wisdom, we have seen enough "spiritually advanced" people with very evident clay (or cloven) feet, and know that they, too, are as subject as the rest of us to the temptations of power, money, sex, and fear. To imagine what they would do with the reins of government is a frightening prospect. We mistrust fascisms, and the Platonic Republic, with its martial guardians and rigid controls, seems fascistic. Democracy has persuaded us that we ourselves know what is best for the body politic, and that we have the right to elect leaders who will execute our choices.

These are some of the grounds for the instinctive rejection of the Platonic political ideal—never mind that the objections too are subject to cynical review. The second main reason comes from Christianity, which began by being antihierarchical and socially leveling. The Jesus of Luke's Gospel, for example, is always giving preference to those at the bottom of the pyramid (women, lepers, the poor,

Samaritans, etc.) and promising a reversal of status in the kingdom of heaven. This accords with the doctrine already mentioned as integral to the Platonic philosophy: that every man and woman is a microcosm, with not only a body and a soul but also an immortal *nous* (consciousness) with its potential for knowing the One. Some have then drawn the conclusion that earthly distinctions are unjust, and that since everyone is a child of God, all should be entitled to an equal voice in the community.

Everyone may be a child of God, but most of these children are very young and have much to learn before they can safely be entrusted with the dangerous toys of government. As Plato pointed out, and as modern history has confirmed, with the best of intentions they will elect a tyrant to lord it over them. This may not be obvious in the democratic West, unless it is realized that elected politicians no longer represent the people who voted for them, but the patrons that enabled them to get elected. Today's tyrants are the special-interests lobbies, the military, legal, and medical industries, the bankers and speculators, the multinationals, etc. These are the operators of the cave system today. It is in their interest to keep most of us fairly prosperous, contented, and dumb, and the show that they put on is quite enough to occupy the minds and emotions of their flock. Yet even some sheep will escape, some worms will turn, and all tyrannies eventually crumble.

6

The Power of the Egregore

L ike the preclassical Greeks, the ancient Romans were
extremely religious, with a kind of animism in which
the whole world was experienced as ensouled.[1] Each
mountain and lake had its spirit; each tree, each family,
home, and hearth was inhabited by an unseen power. All
activities were sacralized, ranging from war and harvest to
childbirth, prophecy, and the common acts of daily life.
There was a right and a wrong way to perform each action,
and success or failure would follow accordingly.[2]

The relics of this old religion were preserved with rev-
erent awe long after the once-struggling city-state had swallowed up most of the known world. The guardians of the
sacred traditions included the Vestal Virgins, the Salii or
leaping priests, the colleges of Augurs and Arvales, and the
supreme office of the Pontifex Maximus, all of whom dis-
charged their duties under the strictest rules and regulations.

The destiny of the state and people was considered to be intimately bound up with these traditional institutions, which had little to fear from, and little effect on, the importation of foreign divinities.

Now if Plato was right, as discussed in the previous chapter, and the visible world is but a shadow of a world more real and more perfect, there is a value and a profound truth in such a religion as the old Romans had. The sacralization of the world and of the conduct of life is a perpetual reminder of immaterial realities and of the priority of the unseen over the seen. But in ancient Rome, at any rate, this did not lead to a world-rejecting attitude: on the contrary, it served as a moral backbone to the state during the difficult centuries of the Republic (509–27 B.C.), fostering the virtues of patriotism, family loyalty, stoicism, and self-control for which the Romans, at their best, are celebrated.

Belief in a spiritual dimension to life is so closely identified today with Christianity and other religions of salvation that it is difficult for modern people to imagine it in its pagan form.[3] But it is clear that the majority of Romans (like the Greeks) invested no great hopes in the afterlife. The death of the body led inevitably to the withering away of the soul, as an impotent subject of Pluto's and Persephone's underground kingdom. Individuals might come and go, but the essential survival was that of the Republic, and, within that, of the clans and families which transcended their individual members. Each of these groups had its presiding and protecting divinities, with whom proper relations were maintained by observance of the rituals.

If one assumes, as the old pagans did and as modern occultists[4] still do, that all earthly things and actions have their nonmaterial correspondences, then there must be a science that studies these and a technology that exploits them. The best-known branch of that technology is ritual, which can be religious (like a mass or a sacrifice), magical (like an invocation), or even secular (like a rally or a procession). Most participants in rituals believe that their actions are a way of propitiating the gods in whom they put their trust. For example, the sacrificial system of the ancient world usually offered the life of an animal in order to obtain a specific benefit from the divinity; and this was as true of Judaism as it was of Greco-Roman paganism.

The skeptic and the philosopher, however, are not content to rest with such an assumption. They may ask awkward questions about who or what this divinity is, whose cooperation is so naïvely assumed by the sacrificer. It is not enough for them to imagine a glorified man or woman sitting up there in Heaven and inhaling the fragrance of burning offal. More often than not, the result of such questioning is disillusionment with the whole system of sacrifice, leading to a more spiritual conception of the divinity, and a more ethical view of human duties. As the Psalmist says: "Thou desirest not sacrifice, else would I give it: thou delightest not in burnt offering. The sacrifices of God are a broken spirit: a broken and a contrite heart, O God, thou wilt not despise" (Ps. 51:16–17).

The matter appears somewhat differently to the student of esotericism and occult philosophy. If earthly things and actions have correspondences of a non-material kind, it may be that the former are not just passive with regard to the latter. The "gods," whatever they may be, may need sacrifices and rituals even more than the worshiper needs the gods.

Such human activities may be the main, even the only, source of their reality. There is an occult concept of the "egregore," a term derived from the Greek word for "watcher."[5] It is used for an immaterial entity that "watches" or presides over some earthly affair or collectivity. The important point is that an egregore is augmented by human belief, ritual, and especially by sacrifice. If it is sufficiently nourished by such energies, the egregore can take on a life of its own and appear to be an independent, personal divinity, with a limited power on behalf of its devotees and an unlimited appetite for their further devotion. It is then believed to be an immortal god or goddess, an angel, or a daimon.

If we consider the old Roman religion in the light of this theory, it may appear as a deliberate strategy to cultivate the egregore of the city-state, in a pact of mutual benefit to the entity and its subjects. Other city-states were evidently doing the same thing, and sometimes warring on one another; but scuffles between gods are nothing new in the pagan mythologies. What is probably new to some readers is the suggestion that there may be an immaterial reality behind these states, nations and families. To ensoul the earth is one thing, leading to comforting ideas of Gaia and Mother Nature. But to ensoul a nation, a race, or a dynasty takes one into disturbing realms of speculation.

One may deoccultize the theory of the egregore by imagining these entities to be mere energy patterns reinforced by use, analogous to the way in which patterns of neurons in the brain are reinforced and strengthened by use and mental effort. The formation of language is one example of how such a pattern may come to form the dominant matrix for our entire human experience. On the collective level, then, I suggest that the old Roman gods and goddesses did have a certain limited reality, and that they were kept alive by the beliefs of the people, the rituals of the priests and priestesses, and psychic energy released and directed in a myriad of animal sacrifices. So long as this compact continued, the egregores watched over the city, which flourished under their protection.

All this would change when the Romans, with the tolerance natural to polytheists, allowed their empire to become the playground for exotic cults and mystery religions, thereby sowing the seeds of their own decline. So, at any rate, thought Edward Gibbon, author of *The Decline and Fall of the Roman Empire*.[6] He blamed the fall of Rome chiefly on the triumph of Christianity; but that was only one of many religions of salvation that were popular during the early centuries of our era. As the empire spread around the Mediterranean, the gods and goddesses of the colonies invaded their host. Orpheus and Dionysus came from Thrace, Demeter from Eleusis, Mithras from Persia, Isis and Serapis from Egypt, Attis and Cybele from Syria, and of course Jesus from Palestine. What distinguished these Mystery religions was the prospect they held out to their initiates of a personal relationship with the divine, and the promise of eternal life.

The influx of the Mystery religions and their doctrines of personal salvation sapped at the foundations of the original Roman mysteries. Once a person is persuaded that he or she can survive death and pass into another and a better life, then the city and its fate must take second place. This is especially the case when the new religion is an initiatic one, requiring deep commitment and offering, in return, membership of an elite group both on earth and in heaven. Sometimes a compromise is possible, as was the case in the mystery religion of Mithras that was so popular among soldiers of the Roman army.[7] In Mithraism it was the virtues of the warrior that led to salvation; and these naturally contributed to the benefit of the state as well as to that of the individual. But a religion whose emphasis was on emotional catharsis, like the cults of Attis and Dionysus, or a religion with revolutionary social ideas, like Christianity, was of no use whatever for sustaining the Empire.

As the centuries of the Christian era progressed, an attempt was made to fortify the Roman egregore through the deification of the Emperors and the establishment of the imperial cult. This became a kind of umbrella religion under which the mass of lesser cults could continue, both in Rome and abroad. But there was a hollow and insincere quality to it, as there always is when a state religion is artificially imposed. The most obvious modern example is the atheistic religion of Communism, which was supposed to sweep the world with enthusiasm for its ideals; but few people really loved it, and around 1989 its egregore slumped from starvation. While the cults of the Roman emperors were splendidly celebrated, it is hard to imagine many people preferring them over the tried and true divinities of the city. The emperors in question were mostly unlovable men, while the philosophical ones, such as Hadrian and Marcus Aurelius, were skeptical about the whole system.

It may be that for a society to flourish, it has to keep its egregore alive; and that for this to happen, the emotional and spiritual focus of the population must be on this world rather than on the next. When they become too interested in their own posthumous salvation, their ancestry becomes less important than their personal fate. State and family become a mere background to their personal quest, helpful or unhelpful as the case may be. I would not suggest for a moment that the triumph of Christianity over the Roman Empire was a triumph for the principles of the Rabbi of Nazareth: those had been thrown overboard long before (starting with Paul of Tarsus). But a religion whose founder showed distinct contempt for power, wealth, family, and social hierarchy was not designed to prop up an overextended empire. Also, as in the case of the other Mystery religions, single-minded devotion to a god or goddess, coupled with the hope of union with him or her after death, seriously diminished the energy left for the traditional egregore to feed upon. By the end of the Roman Empire no one believed any longer in the old gods, and in consequence they withered away.[8] But the egregore of the Empire itself migrated to the Orthodox and Catholic churches, transforming them in the process into pseudoempires of their own.

I have been using the example of ancient Rome to put forward a view of history based on assumptions that are neither materialistic nor conventionally religious. I am suggesting that the rise and fall of nations is intimately bound up with their relations with their gods; and that these are real entities, even though they are not the eternal and all-powerful beings they are reputed to be. This seems to me a theory worthy of consideration by anyone who can admit that the universe is a very strange place, and that there is plenty of room in it for beings bigger than mankind. If such beings exist, it is only prudent to take account of them. Every civilization in the past has done so, after its fashion.[9]

At this point of our study, we have some understanding of the two great matters, or mysteries, with which esotericists of all times and places have concerned themselves. One of these is the mystery of the individual: what the human being is, and what its capacities and prospects are. The crucial issue, towards which many esoteric and occult practices are aimed, is that of death and the possible survival of the personality. It is a mystery because its comprehension is impossible within the boundaries of the logical mind and the sense-bound imagination; but that is not to say that there is no answer to it. The Mystery religions of the ancient world claimed to have found this answer. The second matter is the political mystery: how societies are formed, how they are energized, and what they do with that energy. This is where the egregores come in, together with the human groups that seek to control and manipulate them. Whether they actually do so is another question; I am not encouraging credulity or conspiracy theory, just explaining how they see themselves. Before the age of Greek skepticism, the colleges of priests in ancient Rome truly believed themselves to be the guardians of the Republic and the regulators of relations between its gods and its inhabitants. The same was true of Egypt, ancient Israel, Persia, Vedic India, China, and the theocracies of Mexico and Peru. All of these had a theology that was not abstract or merely verbal, as the discipline is today, but severely practical, and controlled by a jealously close-knit college of priests.

The next chapter will examine some of the tensions between the individual and the political mysteries as they erupted in antiquity and the early Middle Ages.

The Meddling God

During the early centuries A.D., when the Hermetic treatises were being written and the Neoplatonists were reviving Plato's teachings, a number of schools or sects appeared under the banner of "gnosis," or the true knowledge that leads to salvation.[1] What was this "true knowledge"? It was nothing new. Plato explains in Book Six of his *Republic* that there are four levels of knowing.[2] The first is the inner perception of our own imaginations.[3] Second is the opinions that we base on the evidence of the senses.[4] Third is the more accurate knowledge obtained through rational thought.[5] And the fourth, to which later Greeks gave the name of gnosis,[6] is the direct knowledge of spiritual reality, which brings a certainty even beyond reason.

Anyone can experience the fourth type of knowledge instantly, if not very usefully, by asking themselves: "Do I exist?" It is so obvious, so intimate a fact that one never thinks to question it. The knowledge given in gnosis is like that. Another classic example is the answer that Carl Jung (1875–1961), the great Gnostic of the twentieth century, gave to the BBC television interviewer who asked him if he believed in God: "I do not believe; I know."[7]

If only we could all have gnosis, and know the nature of things without fumbling with opinions and logic-chopping! It seems rather unfair that we are denied it, since it is evidently within the human capacity. The are examples, admittedly rare, of quite ordinary people who have suddenly been opened permanently to the gnostic dimension. Douglas Harding[8] and John Wren-Lewis[9] come to mind. As they describe the experience, they go on living their lives and dealing with the same problems as the rest of us (human relations, money, illness, etc.), but against a background of serene and perfect certainty that all of life is a play, and that they are one with the Player.

Wren-Lewis, reflecting on his sudden and unplanned opening to the gnostic dimension, speculated that long ago people were all in this state, and that it is our natural human birthright. This is certainly a stimulus for speculation about human ancestry. Perhaps the great brain of Neanderthal man—larger than mine or yours—served for modes of knowing that totally elude us. As it is, we are using only a fraction of our cerebrum.[10] For all we know, the rest of it holds the potential of knowledge that transcends the senses and language, and is hence incommunicable and unimaginable to those who lack this knowledge.

But this is to argue from the physical to the metaphysical, whereas most authorities on gnosis go the opposite way, blaming the physical body for the frustration of our spiritual potential. Plato, influenced by the Orphic and Pythagorean *soma-sema* doctrine (see chapter 4) wrote that "the body is a tomb for the soul."[11] He seemed to blame the body for our ignorant predicament, and recommended philosophy as the means of separating ourselves from it.[12] The ultimate philosophic ideal would then be the Hermetic ascent of the soul through the cosmic spheres[13] (as described in chapter 2), which disburdens the soul of all the bad tendencies it has acquired through falling into matter. At the end of the ascent, which can be accomplished in initiation and not merely after death, the purified soul regains its pristine state and enters the realm of the gods. But even then, the chances are that the cycle will be reenacted, for the soul has an inexplicable lust for the body, and cannot resist plunging into it if the chance is offered.[14]

A majority of the Gnostic schools, not content with the quest for liberation through knowledge of the Real, shared a cosmology that was supposed to explain why we have lost it. They attributed the existence of the material world to an evil and inferior member of the heavenly hierarchy called the Demiurge. That was originally Plato's name for the god who has constructed the physical world, as a deputy from the supreme One.[15] For Plato and his school, the world and the bodies made from its matter are not evil, but on the contrary very beautiful; they are just low down on the cosmic ladder which the philosopher aspires to climb. For Gnosticism, on the contrary, the world is a catastrophic mistake made by a malevolent junior god who thinks that he is supreme and tyrannizes over a host of souls entrapped in bodies.[16] Plato's attitude was hierarchical; Gnosticism's was dualistic. That was what was novel about the movement.

Arising in the context of a Christianity ill at ease with its Judaic origins, Gnosticism offered the most radical solution to the problem by casting the Hebrew god Yahweh in the role of this malevolent Demiurge.[17] If Yahweh had not actually created the physical world (and Gnostic schools differ on this detail), he and his evil Archons had held it in their grip for thousands of years, nourished by the devotion of his chosen people and their animal sacrifices. All of this had confirmed his illusion, or the illusion that it suited him to maintain in his followers: that he was himself the One God, Lord of the Universe and maker of all things.

Unknown, no doubt, to the majority of its readers, this Gnostic notion dominates the third novel of Philip Pullman's great fantasy trilogy, *The Amber Spyglass*.[18] Here the Ancient of Days and his lieutenant Metatron have kept the souls of the dead imprisoned in their egos in a dreary, harpy-guarded limbo. After the defeat of the tyrants, the hero and heroine liberate the dead by releasing their energies back to Nature, just as in the *Poimandres* "your vital spirit you yield up to the atmosphere, so that it no longer works in you; and the bodily senses go back to their own sources, becoming parts of the universe, and entering into fresh combinations to do other work."[19]

Then, the Gnostic myth continues, came Jesus, sent as an emissary from the True God to abrogate Yahweh's meaningless laws and to show select human souls the way of escape.[20] And the way lies not though love, or morality, but only through gnosis: the direct knowledge that the Demiurge has been at pains to suppress in us, but which can still be kindled by the spark of divinity that lies buried in us all.

There is no intrinsic need to link the doctrine of saving knowledge with a dualistic worldview. The possibility of gnosis also exists in Platonism, Hermetism, and for that matter in Kabbalah, Sufism, Hinduism, and Buddhism, none of which has a dualistic theology. It is simply because some of the principal Gnostic sects were dualistic that their "gnosis"-derived name has become a label for this particular doctrine of the Demiurge.

After the fall of the Roman Empire in the fifth century A.D., these two main features of Gnostic philosophy continued to flourish in the Middle East, though no longer united as they had been in classic Gnosticism. The esoteric teaching of a way of salvific knowledge continued in Persia, where the native Zoroastrian tradition welcomed the last of the Neoplatonists. The Zoroastrian philosophers had already developed a complex system of angels, worlds, and states of the soul in which these things were known. They also had a personification of evil, Ahriman, but he was certainly not the creator of the world, only its spoiler. The higher one goes in Zoroastrian theosophy, the further one is from Gnostic dualism. It was perilous to maintain this initiatic and mystical school in the face of the Islamic invasion and conversion of Persia. Nevertheless, an accommodation was made with the Qur'anic teachings that allowed an Islamic theosophic tradition to survive for many centuries, and to produce an incomparable wealth of inspired writings, colorful angelic visions, and detailed bulletins from the immaterial world that is the object of gnosis. During the Dark Ages of Europe, the light of wisdom was burning brightly in Persia.[21]

Gnostic dualism, on the other hand, had flourished in the religion of Manichaeism, founded by the Jewish-Christian Mani near Babylon in the third century. In Mani's theology, the Evil God is not a misguided underling of the One, but a high power in his own right and the eternal rival of the Good God. We have our spirits from the Good God, but our bodies from the Evil one. Jesus and the other prophets, says Manichaean doctrine, have come to offer us the saving gnosis that releases our spirits from bondage, so that we can rejoin the Good and abandon the Evil one to the dead world he has created.

Manichaeism survived during the Dark Ages in the Near East and in Eastern Europe, where it took on new names and forms and periodically emerged to aggravate the established churches. The Bogomils ("beloved of God") of Thrace or Bulgaria were one such offshoot, first entering the historical record in the tenth century.[22] Their theology laid the blame for the world's evil on God's firstborn son, called Satanael, who rebelled against his father, then came down to earth with his rebel angels and seduced Eve: their child was Cain. In due course, Satanael persuaded the Jews that he was the Supreme God, and gave Moses a law of his own devising. Jesus was an emissary from the Supreme God, who after his resurrection took Satanael's vacant seat in heaven. The Bogomils denied most of the Church's dogmas and despised its practices, leading an ascetic and ethical life. Like many heretical sects, they considered themselves the only true believers, or to be precise, the only ones who had not been fooled by the Evil One.

The Bogomils illustrate a syndrome common to esoteric groups as well as to more exoteric cults: a conviction that they have a deeper or a truer knowledge than the established churches, and that they thereby stand apart from the deluded mass of humanity. However, measured against Plato's definitions of the levels of knowledge, theirs was only a pseudognosis, being just as much based on opinion and politics as any religious dogma.

Something of the Bogomils and their doctrine survived, to resurface in the Cathars of northern Italy and southern France. It was never clearly established whether they considered the evil world-creator as equal to or dependent from the True God. But they certainly believed that the Roman Church, with its unchristian wealth and abuses, belonged in the Demiurge's camp.

The Cathars were Gnostic dualists, but without a concept of gnosis as the way of salvation. Instead, they practiced a sacramental laying on of hands. They aspired to a sexless, vegetarian life, in order to deny the Demiurge anything connected with physical reproduction and birth in his world of matter. But, realizing that not everyone is capable of asceticism, they allowed for an exoteric body of more worldly "believers" beside the esoteric "true Christians." The Cathars also had their bishops and clergy, and held most of the Languedoc region (Provence) under their influence. Until the early thirteenth century, when the pope and the mercenaries of the king of France mounted a genocidal "crusade" against them, theirs was one of the most civilized and artistic corners of Europe.

Perhaps it is merely temperament that decides whether one divides the universe of one's experience into higher and lower, or into good and evil. Gnostic dualism in its many forms certainly attracts those who are looking for somewhere to place the blame for an imperfect world. And if the blame can be placed on that which someone else regards as most holy, there is the additional thrill—for those of a certain temperament—of insulting or degrading them. There is no room here for an analysis of modern groups that wear the Gnostic label,[23] but one could begin by sorting them into those primarily inspired by the quest for spiritual gnosis and those centered on dualism and the revolt against the Church, seen as an extension of the Demiurge's power.

That said, the science fiction scenario of Gnosticism is not to be dismissed lightly. There are scientists today who believe and even hope that the human race will eventually take over other planets and exploit their environments, with any life forms that may be found there, for human advantage. Give us a million more years and we might become an evil Demiurge ourselves, enslaving the inhabitants of some hapless planetary system, perhaps even without their knowledge. In an era of genetic manipulations, it is no longer frivolous to wonder whether our own earth, and our bodies, might have suffered some such intervention by beings cleverer than ourselves. Mythological and esoteric literature has many suggestions of this kind, though unsubtle minds like Erich von Däniken[24] and his millions of readers have dragged the issue down to the lowest level of "gods from outer space," thus isolating it from intelligent discourse.

I think that it is time to dust off the Gnostic mythology and to reconsider it in a dispassionate frame of mind. There are two questions to be considered. The first is the epistemological one: does the human being have a potential for gnosis, and if so, how do we recognize it? Obviously we cannot believe everyone who goes around claiming to possess higher knowledge. I suspect that the answer to this question may reside purely in the subjective domain: that the person who has it, knows it, but that it is incommunicable and perhaps even useless to anyone else.[25] To cite the example at the beginning of this chapter, I may know that I exist, but that doesn't prove to you that I do!

The second question is the historical one of whether the human race may have undergone interference from outside in the distant past. In view of the continuing inability of materialistic science to explain the origins of humanity,[26] it seems worth collecting material bearing on this hypothesis.[27] As a corollary, one might include the theory of the egregore, mentioned in the previous chapter: the theory that there exist immaterial energy complexes that are sustained by human beliefs and emotions, and consequently assume a quasi-independent, personal guise. The powerful effects of egregores over collective behavior range from what the Victorian author Charles Mackay called "extraordinary popular delusions and the madness of crowds" up to entire religious movements, which dissolve as soon as their energy sources are cut off. Perhaps there is no more to the evil Demiurge than that; perhaps the fantasies about him derive from the collective energies that compel people, in the mass, to do stupid and cruel things which they conveniently blame on a "god."

8

The Negative Theology

The Dark Ages knew of no mystery schools such as had flourished in Antiquity. The Pythagorean and Orphic brotherhoods, the Platonic Academy, the Hermetic and Mithraic cults—all had disappeared from Europe along with the Roman Empire. Their vision of man as a microcosm, reflecting in miniature the whole universe and its source, and their offer of a path by which man could become divine, were almost lost. The new official religion of Christianity could barely tolerate such ideas, even among its own intellectual elite. The Church's power rested on the divinity of one man only, Jesus Christ, and on one path to salvation for the rest: that of obedience.

Despite this we can sometimes glimpse, like a golden thread half buried in the soil, the legacy of a Christian theosophic tradition that was very different from the mainstream. This seems to have derived its energy from mystical experience, weighed and interpreted in the light of Neo-platonic philosophy. What characterizes this tradition is that it does not assert anything about God, but rather denies the possibility of assertion. It is the antithesis of the type of utterance that begins: "Thus saith the Lord." It grew quite naturally out of Neoplatonism, when an unidentified Greek writer known as Dionysius the Areopagite[1] reinter-preted the highest flights of pagan mysticism in the light of the new religion.

Dionysius was well aware of the dangers of exoteric monotheism. He deplored those "who describe the tran-scendental First Cause of all by characteristics derived from the lowest order of beings."[2] His best efforts to describe it worthily take the form of paradoxes, or of statements of what it is not (hence "negative theology"). He speaks of it as outshining all brilliance with the intensity of its darkness; as possessing all the attributes of the universe, since it is the universal cause of all, yet possessing none of them since it transcends them all.[3]

The words of theologians tend to be dry, but here they spring from a direct experience that is, paradoxically, no experience, because there is no separate self to experience it. Dionysius says in another paradox, sounding just like Plotinus: "Through the inactivity of all his reasoning pow-ers the mystic is united by his highest faculty to That which is wholly unknowable; thus by knowing nothing he knows That which is beyond knowledge."[4]

These things, Dionysius says, are not to be disclosed to the uninitiated.[5] In fact they were disclosed, and served as inspiration to the entire Christian mystical tradition. Beside his *Mystical Theology*, from which these quotes are taken,

Dionysius wrote a treatise, *On the Celestial Hierarchies,* that is the foundation of all Christian angel lore. His achievement was to make the principles of Neoplatonic theology acceptable to monotheism. He reclassified the hierarchies of gods and daimons as the Nine Orders of Angels,[6] and made them accord with Hebrew tradition and with the Bible. Thus the hierarchy of secondary powers who rule the cosmos[7] was saved from extinction in the imagination of the new era.

Dionysius's double achievement makes him the father of Christian esotericism.[8] First, he teaches that the Absolute is indescribable and utterly transcendent, yet in some way accessible and present in man. This is the ultimate justification for every spiritual effort. Then he fills in the rest of the cosmic hierarchy, populating the heavens and the spheres with invisible beings. These become the foundation of ceremonial magic, philosophical astrology, a revived Hermetic cosmology, and hence of the occult sciences in Europe.

Dionysius was unknown in the West until the ninth century, when the Irish monk John Scotus Eriugena translated his works into Latin. Eriugena then developed the anonymous theosopher's principles into a grandiose conception of the universe and human destiny. A natural Platonist, he saw no difference between true religion and true philosophy, because the entire conceivable universe— the object of philosophic speculation—is inseparable from God. What one might call Eriugena's "positive theology" concerns Nature, seen as God in the process of self–revelation. Thanks to this, humans are also able to become God, or sons of God. What is more, in the end all of them will be redeemed, along with all the animals and even the devils. This kindly doctrine of Eriugena's was in stark contrast to the eternal Hell favored, or feared, by orthodox believers.[9]

The other aspect of God is the negative or indescribable one, but to Eriugena this is paradoxically also accessible, by the very fact that we are all divine in our inmost natures. He says in his *Homily on the Prologue to St. John's Gospel*: "John, therefore, was not a human being but more than a human being when he flew above himself and all things which are. Transported by the ineffable power of wisdom and by purest keenness of mind, he entered into that which is beyond all things. . . . He would not have been able to ascend into God if he had not first become God."[10]

The third great proponent of the negative theology is Meister Eckhart (c. 1260–1327), another keen reader of Dionysius.[11] Eckhart was no hermit but a capable monastic administrator in Bohemia and Germany. Far from reserving his teachings to an esoteric few, he proclaimed them to the world. He preached his sermons not in learned Latin, but in the powerful and earthy monosyllables of his native Rhineland.

Eckhart's main theme was the potential of man to know, and in a way to be, God. He told his listeners that when a man abides in God, "there is no difference between him and God; they are one." Here is one of his explanations of why this is so: "When God created man he safeguarded him against all ills; the golden chain of destiny coming from the Trinity to the highest power of the soul and running also through her lower powers subordinates them to the higher so that no fell disorder can attack either the body or the soul excepting he transgress this law. In her higher powers the soul is spirit and in her lower, soul; and betwixt soul and spirit is the bond of one common being."[12]

Meister Eckhart here suggests a threefold analysis of the human being as consisting of spirit, soul, and body, with spirit (*Geist* in his German—like the "Holy Ghost" in older English texts) at the head of the hierarchy. Such an arrangement had been present in Platonism, but was not part of regular Christian doctrine, which with rare exceptions allows man a soul and body only.[13] The Latin term *spiritus* is used for the Holy Spirit, but otherwise applied to a much lower order of invisible beings and substances[14] (again, compare the uses of the word "ghost"). When reading esoteric theories about the constitution of man, it is important to know how the author is using the word "spirit": either as something more divine than the soul, or merely for the subtle link between soul and body.

Eckhart's concept of threefold man is also the foundation of spiritual alchemy (see chapter 13), in which Sulphur and Mercury symbolize spirit, in the higher sense, and soul. Their conjunction or "chemical wedding" then represents the union of the entire soul with its highest, spiritual principle,[15] i.e., with the divinity within, which is indistinguishable from the God who can only be described in negations.

Of these three theologians, Dionysius eluded official censure because he was believed to have been a companion of St. Paul, as well as the patron saint of France. Eriugena's writings were condemned by several church councils, mainly on the grounds of pantheism (making a god out of the universe). Meister Eckhart was excommunicated in 1329, shortly after his death, when he could no longer answer the charges made against him: these included proclaiming the secrets of the Church to the public. And indeed he had done so, wisely or unwisely sharing the inner certainties of one "from whom God hid nothing."

Christianity has always had problems with its mystics and theosophers, because they cannot help straying from the path laid out for the great mass of the faithful.[16] With very rare exceptions, of which Socrates is the most famous, this problem did not arise in polytheistic cultures. It is a symptom of the contradiction that lies at the heart of monotheistic religions. Semitic monotheism, often celebrated as a great advance in the history of religious ideas, was actually a retrograde step in almost every respect. It illustrates how a truth, when transposed to the wrong level, can spawn a host of false concepts in the exoteric mind.

The subtle intelligence of Indian, Egyptian, and Greek philosophers easily grasped the truth of monotheism: that there can be only one ultimate source of all things. But the ordinary worshipper, in every religion, takes comfort not from metaphysics but from faith, and draws spiritual sustenance from a personal relationship with a god or goddess. A polytheistic culture like ancient Rome or modern India recognizes that there are many worthy objects for such devotion, and allows everyone his or her divinity of choice. Its philosophers keep their understanding to themselves, and do not interfere in people's religious customs by saying: "You should throw down the idols of Jupiter (Shiva, Isis, etc.) and worship the ineffable One!" Not so the monotheisms. The scriptures of Judaism, Christianity, and Islam insist that there is only one God, and in a sense they are right. But what they call God is no longer the One of the philosophers. He is a masculine entity with attributes of a far lower order, such as tribal chauvinism, the desire for love, response to prayers and bribery, and intervention in human affairs. He is no better than the gods of Olympus, yet he is supposed to be the source of all. And as he acts, with bitter enmity to the worshipers of other gods, so do his followers—as if the One could care!

I cannot blame Christ, or the esoteric school that originated the Christian mythology, for the millennium and a half of heresy–hunting, schisms, persecutions, inquisitions, and civil wars waged in his name. I can only blame the "one way" mentality, which leads to rigidity, dogmatism, and the conviction that it has a monopoly of the truth, backed by an anthology of Hebrew and Greek writings still held by many people to be the Word of God. When the cause of these terrors was not basely political or economic, it stemmed from someone's conviction that he possessed some truth about God which his opponents disputed or denied. Few things are more dangerous in human affairs, or have such painful consequences, than the religious person's conviction of his own rightness. The conviction of Dionysius, Eriugena, Eckhart, and the like was of an entirely different order. But once they descended from the heights of metaphysical contemplation, they too could not avoid using the imagery, and eventually the dogmas, that Church and Bible had instilled in them. Dionysius, for example, wrote a companion volume to his *Celestial Hierarchy* in which he defended the ecclesiastical hierarchy of bishops, priests, and deacons on the grounds that it reflected the orders of angels. Eriugena, for all his unitive vision of God and Nature, felt obliged to attack the Arian heresy, which holds that the Son is not equal to the Father, as well as the theologies of the

Jews and pagans. Eckhart strove to extract hidden meanings from every phrase of Scripture, with touching confidence that its authors were more divinely inspired even than himself. The same relationship to revealed writings existed in the other monotheisms. In the medieval Islamic world there were mystics of no lesser distinction than the Christian ones, for whom everything, apart from the unknowable God, appeared in the theological categories of the Qur'an, which expresses horror that God should be said to bring forth a Son.[17] And the enlightened masters of Kabbalah, who felt authorized to speak of the *Ain*—the indescribable plenitude of Nothingness—did not believe that they had come to it through the grace of Jesus Christ.

How can we deal with these staring differences at the most fundamental level of faith, touching on the very essence of theology, which divide the three Abrahamic religions from each other? Only in a postreligious age can we begin to contemplate an answer, and the answer I propose will not be acceptable to many. I suggest that the indescribable experiences of these mystics be taken as the best evidence we have of the central truth of monotheism: that there is one reality behind and beyond all things, to which the human being is mysteriously connected. But the sacred and revealed books, the contentious theologies, the laws, clergy, and qualified images of God seem to me proof positive of the central truth of polytheism: that there are many higher beings than us in the universe, some of whom enter into relations with mankind. Gods and goddesses, angels and daimons, spirits, egregores, or extraterrestrials—classify them as you will. The matter is probably very complex and beyond our categories of thought.[18] But it is these beings, I suspect, that are responsible for the "revealed" religions and for the mutual exchange of energy that keeps them, against all probability, alive.

Cathedrals of Light

*T*he previous chapter touched on some of the troubles caused by people who think that they know something about God: not people like Dionysius the Areopagite, John Scotus Eriugena, or Meister Eckhart, who insisted that God is indescribable, but the "positive theologians" who are so prone to argue with each other. Perhaps the trouble really comes from using words, which are so inadequate for the purpose because they reflect the constructs and the limitations of rational, left–brain consciousness.

There is no such dispute when the other side of the brain is engaged, as by sounds, shapes, colors—in short, by beauty. The appreciation of the world's beauty and the joy of adding to it, as far as humans are able, is another constant thread, sometimes running parallel to the one we are following in this book. One such case is the Gothic cathedrals.

If you have ever traveled to one of the great cathedral towns of Europe, you will know the experience of seeing the cathedral first, from a distance, before the town comes into sight. It dwarfs every other human contribution to the landscape, and the contrast was all the greater at the time it was built. The towers and spires point to heaven as a symbol of aspiration to God. But they could also be seen as lightning-rods, drawing down celestial influences into the soil. In either sense, the cathedral, with its unearthly bulk and height, seems to loom somewhere between heaven and earth.

In quantitative terms, the Gothic cathedrals are as astonishing as the Pyramids. In France alone, the ninety years from 1180 to 1270 saw the building of eighty cathedrals and nearly five hundred abbeys. The whole country's economy was dominated by it. The only comparison today would be with the arms race, for which the people of Third World countries sacrifice so much. But a cathedral also made money, attracting merchants to fairs on the Church's feast days, and hordes of pilgrims allured by relics. Rather than being the silent sanctuary or tourist trap of today, it teemed with real life, serving as emporium, school, court of justice, labor exchange, and even dormitory.

We are more concerned here with its qualitative aspect, and with the Gothic cathedral as evidence for the hidden wisdom that has been passed down the ages. Such a project summons the efforts of the entire community, but the original concept is not created by democratic debate, neither is the design. These require specialized knowledge and a power of creative imagination that we sometimes call "genius."

What was the ultimate purpose of a Gothic cathedral? It was a finely tuned vehicle for getting souls to heaven. Those who conceived it, and those who used it, considered the unseen world much more important than the world of the senses. Without this set of priorities, they would never have put so much energy into the cult of relics, the custom of pilgrimage, and the generous giving to sacred causes. The cathedral was a temporary reward to them for their devotion. Dominating the material world both physically and economically, like the skyscraper canyons of Wall Street, it also offered (unlike them) a foretaste of the joys of heaven.

Dionysius the Areopagite, the Christian Platonist who founded the school of "negative theology," was also a metaphysician of light.[1] Though the Godhead in itself is a thrice-unknown darkness, when it manifests a universe the first apparition is the divine light. The first chapters of Genesis and St. John's Gospel are explicit on this point. To Dionysius, the light that we know on earth is the clearest sensory echo of that first creation. The divine ray shines down from the Father and flows into us, filling us with memory of the things above and leading us back to unity with God.

The Gothic cathedrals may seem dusky today, lit only by their stained–glass windows. But in comparison with the earlier Romanesque style, they were flooded with light. For this we may thank Suger, abbot of Saint–Denis, who rebuilt his own abbey in the mid–twelfth century while enraptured by the light–mysticism of Dionysius, and thereby launched the Gothic style.[2] Suger's declared intention was to fill the building with the most divine substance in existence. He wrote: "Brightly shines that which multiplies brightness;

and bright is the noble work through which the new light shines"³— the latter also alluding to Christ, the Light of the World.

Gothic illumination was neither the white purity we prefer today, nor the brightly painted walls of the earlier, Romanesque style, but the rainbow colors made possible by recent advances in glassmaking. For the first time in history, people were able to experience on a large scale the effects of direct, colored light, as opposed to the reflected light of paintings, flowers, etc. Modern experiments in light therapy show that this exposure has a definite psychophysical effect. Today's sensitive visitor to the cathedrals hardly needs to be told that, much less the people for whom analogies like Suger's were at the center of their being. How could they not think of the New Jerusalem, with its walls compounded from twelve different gemstones, lit by the light of the Lamb? (Rev. 21:19–22).

Before the Gothic cathedrals began to rise, northern France was already home to a unique school of spiritual philosophy, the Cathedral School of Chartres. They were readers of Dionysius and Eriugena, and also of Plato and the Neoplatonists—what little they could find of them before the influx of Greek manuscripts in the Renaissance. In a partial Latin version of Plato's *Timaeus* they had read about how the cosmos was created, not through light but through the power of number and geometry. Timaeus, who speaks most of the dialogue, was a Pythagorean, and he puts forward the view of his school that the ultimate realities of the creation are mathematical numbers and geometrical forms. The elements and everything made from them come into being through their combinations.

The Chartres philosophers had almost as much respect for Plato's creation myth as for the one in Genesis. It had the allure of being a rational system, which man might have a chance of understanding; it made God a rational being. Besides, the Book of Wisdom had said: "Thou hast created all things in number and weight and measure" (Wisd. of Sol. 11:20). So God the Father was sometimes depicted in manuscripts as the Geometer, mapping out the cosmos with a pair of compasses.[4] The Mystery of the Trinity, said one Chartres master,[5] is like an equilateral triangle—another image often found in manuscripts and paintings. He adds ingeniously that the relation of Jesus to the Father is like the first square number, 1 x 1 = 1: they remain in unity.

Geometry and number are the first principles of any building, even a garden shed. In order to get built, it has to have a shape, and it must be measured. The cathedrals—and this includes the Romanesque and Byzantine ones, not just the Gothic—are the supreme human effort to imitate God by imposing geometry and number on matter. They are mathematical principles made visible, tangible, and habitable. One can say the same of Egyptian, Greek, and Roman temples, indeed of sacred structures the world over.

There are two main aspects to the mathematics of sacred buildings. The first is the arithmetical one, consisting in the choice of a module (e.g., the foot) and its multiples (e.g., the squares that make up the ground plan). The cathedral builders sometimes chose numbers for their symbolic value. In Chartres, for example, the main dimensions, expressed in the units of the time, correspond to the gematria[6] of expressions like *Beata Virgo Maria Mater Dei* (Blessed Virgin Mary, Mother of God).[7] No one knew this between the time when it was determined by the architect and the time when John James rediscovered it in the 1970s. But that is of no more significance, to the Platonic mentality, than my ignorance of the fine adjustments that make my car or computer work. The cathedral "works" precisely because it is made like that.

The second aspect of sacred mathematics is geometry, which uses the tools of compass and square, whereas arithmetic used the abacus. Arithmetic dictates dimension, geometry, shape; hence it is responsible for the engineering of the building. Will it stay up? That was the main worry of the Gothic architects, who, obedient to the metaphysics of light, opened up their walls to contain ever larger expanses of stained glass. The two–centered or pointed arch was their most notable resource, and the flying buttress their insurance. The tracery of the rose windows was their playground, where they displayed their virtuosity in the symbolic divisions of the circle.

Geometry is partly transposable to arithmetic: a given shape can be assigned definite dimensions. But in part it transcends measurable number. One of the most fascinating problems to ancient mathematicians was the impossibility of arriving at an arithmetical expression for things easily drawn, like a circle or the diagonal of a square, or the infinite expansion of the Golden Section. These irrational proportions also have their place in the design of the cathedrals, and all the more appropriately since they are so conspicuous in the design of the physical cosmos.[8]

Thus far, the cathedral was calculated to be a reflection of God's mathematical intelligence, and a vessel for his first creation of light. One more thing was needed to complete the effect: the cathedral must be made to sound. Then the three primary faculties of mind, eye, and ear could all be satisfied.

I do not mean to suggest that a small group of musicians sat down to determine what sort of music would fit the new architectural style, in analogy with the master–masons and Christian Platonists who undoubtedly devised the fabric of the building. But it is a fact that the music composed for the liturgy at the new cathedral of Notre-Dame became the first international repertory of harmonized music.[9] It spread throughout Europe and served as the foundation and inspiration for the next century's developments,[10] from which a clear line can be traced to the more familiar music, popular and classical alike, whose harmonic nature everyone takes for granted.

Why is harmony important? The Pythagorean musician will answer that it is because through harmony we can perceive the proportions by which the cosmos is created. You can write down the first five numbers, 1, 2, 3, 4, 5: that is arithmetic. You can make structures based on these as dimensions: that is geometry. But if you pluck five strings whose relative lengths are 1, ½, ⅓, ¼, and ⅕, lo and behold—you hear a major chord![11] Harmony is number made audible. Some number combinations produce concords; others discords. And out of the tension between the two types, all our music arises.

Some people maintain that buildings made in harmonic proportions are acoustically better than ones not so designed. The acoustics of the Gothic cathedrals, and also of the innumerable smaller churches built after the same principles, are best suited to the music of earlier periods, which was harmonically simple and intended for unaccompanied voices. Romantic instrumental music (with all due respect to the French organ school)[12] sounds chaotic in them. The reason for the success of the earlier music seems to be that these buildings enhance the natural harmonics that are present in every tone. A mere pair of solo voices singing one of the mass settings of Léonin, the first Notre–Dame composer, take on a rich bouquet of harmonics that fills the whole building.[13] Nothing more was needed to complete the designedly unworldly atmosphere.

The Gothic cathedral was a feast for the senses. I have said little about how it was also a feast for the mind, as the stained–glass windows depicted hundreds of biblical figures, each with his or her own story. Nor have I mentioned the sculptural programs that repeated on the outside of the building the themes that the glass showed on the inside. I have said nothing about the mass, the central mystery of the Christian liturgy, with its magical transubstantiation of bread and wine into Christ's body and blood. For a believer, the miracle of the cathedral, in all its vastness and beauty, was nothing to the daily miracle that took place at its altars. Then there is the theme beloved of modern rediscoverers of the Gothic:[14] the feminine face of Deity represented by the Virgin Mary, whose worship at shrines like Chartres is like a rebirth of the goddess cults of the ancient world.[15] But taking all of this together, we can see how the seeds planted by a few Christian Platonists, nurtured by a few experts in architecture and harmony, grew into one of the greatest adornments of civilization that the world has ever known.

If there is an Invisible College[16] working to enlighten the world, this may have been their best achievement. It served not just the elite and the initiates but all people, touching each one at the appropriate level, from a kind of superstition we can scarcely credit today, up through every degree of religious attunement, to the heights of devotional mysticism. Earlier I called it a finely tuned vehicle for getting souls to heaven. This holds good even if the only heaven that exists is the one that we make on earth.

CHAPTER

10

The Arts of the Imagination

How would you go about building a cathedral in a paperless and largely illiterate society? Modern architects, of course, draw scale diagrams and work out every detail on paper, which then serves to convey their intentions to the builder. But in earlier times all of the planning, from the basic engineering to the decorative motifs, had to be done internally, in the architect's mind. The "masons' secret" of the ancient architect was that he was trained to construct an entire building in his imagination, so that once work began on the site, he could give instructions at every point. By referring to the pattern stored in his memory, the architect could tell the laborers how every stone should be cut and fitted.

The researches of Marsha Keith Schuchard[1] have revealed the astonishing connections of ancient architecture with two systems of mental manipulation: Kabbalistic meditation and the Art of Memory. In retrospect, it makes perfect sense that ancient architects should have developed the technique of active imagination far beyond anything we are capable of today. Also, given that ancient architects, from Stonehenge to Chartres, were primarily engaged with sacred buildings, it is certain that their imaginations were suffused with religious myths and symbols. The mental construction of temples and churches was inseparable from meditation on the meaning of those myths, while the intense effort of imagination could easily pass over into visionary experience.

The twelfth and thirteenth centuries, which saw the rise of the cathedrals in the Christian West, were also golden years for Kabbalists and Sufis. The practice of active imagination is the essence of Kabbalah, in which the mental manipulation of letters, numbers, and geometrical forms in two and three dimensions supposedly leads to the understanding of God's creative plan.[2] This understanding may eventually bring the Kabbalist to the conviction of knowing God. The same techniques were practiced by Sufis, as mentioned in chapter 1.[3]

The Art of Memory, known to the ancients, was allied to these meditative practices, but was specifically architectural: its basic technique was to imagine a building in which symbolic images of the things to be remembered were placed sequentially on the walls and in the rooms.[4] In the Dark Ages of the Christian West it was the Jews and Muslims, often living peacefully side by side, who cultivated such techniques and the worldly skills associated with them: mathematics, architecture, and engineering. These passed, in time, into the Christian world, and came to form part of the secret teachings of the guild of masons, whose imagery betrays its origin by being drawn exclusively from the Old Testament.[5]

The Western esoteric tradition has always emphasized the use of the imagination as the primary way of access to higher worlds. All esoteric schools, as far as I know, train their students in visualization and active imagination (sometimes included within the broader term of "meditation"). The inner senses can be strengthened, just as the muscles of an athlete or the skill of a musician are developed through training. The time, effort, and dedication required are comparable in all three cases, as is the need for a genetic disposition.

Our concern here is both with the esoteric use of the imagination as a vehicle for entering inner worlds, and its exoteric use for education and indoctrination. There are various ways to stimulate the imagination, including fasting, sleep deprivation, and a wide range of drugs. The goal is to overcome its usual imprecision and fuzziness, and to achieve a degree of clarity and reality rivaling that of the waking environment.

The medieval Irish monks were among the first and most enthusiastic explorers of the visionary realm, which they experienced in a mode half-Christianized and half still indebted to the pagan traditions of their land. It was a well-defined "Other World" with its own landmarks and inhabitants, including the fairy folk who found their niche in the Christian cosmology as semifallen angels.[6] Usually the Other World is reached after an imaginary sea voyage to the West. It is as full of adventures as Ireland itself, but more full of holiness, as the voyager often meets unfallen spirits, dwelling in Edenic gardens where they celebrate a liturgy of song and sacred dance. Everything in that world is more crystalline, the fruits more delicious, the beasts and birds more tame and endowed with speech.

Naturally the Irish voyages pass today as fantasy fiction, as does the culmination of all medieval soul journeys: the *Divine Comedy* of Dante (1265–1321). Rational scholarship knows no intermediary between fact and fiction, and since those Western Isles, much less hell, purgatory, and paradise, do not exist, what happens there has to have been invented. But rational scholars are typically unacquainted with the workings of the creative mind. They do not know those ecstasies in which the poet beholds "forms more real than living man,"[7] which he later attempts to capture in verse. If they did, they would call them hallucinations.

The training of the Kabbalists and Sufis, subject as it was to their religious convictions and the teachings of their holy books, led the imaginative voyager to encounter a world with a definite topography and population.[8] Obviously, the Jewish and the Muslim versions differed, except perhaps at the very summit where the angels and their heavens give way to Yahweh, or Allah. But each was consistent. The purpose of visiting them through meditation was the purification of the soul through the experience of higher worlds, not indulgence in the astral Disneyland familiar to the abusers of hallucinogens. The devotees expected to meet with confirmation of their faith, and this, for the most part, they duly received. If their accounts were copied and circulated, it was to encourage others and to reinforce the whole scenario. Awkwardness only occurred when the sublimity of the experience made the voyagers insubordinate to exoteric dogma, so that on coming down to earth they uttered heretical opinions. For such rashness, the Sufis Al-Hallaj and Suhrawardi were executed.[9]

Dante, of course, does not describe a Jewish or a Muslim cosmos, but one based on Christian and especially Scholastic doctrine, and highly colored, especially in the *Inferno*, by his own personal and political agenda. His account is so circumstantial, so vivid, detailed, and poetically memorable, that for centuries it has fed the imaginations of his countrymen. To read Dante, or any other work of the visionary imagination, is to partake in passive mode in the experience, which is all most of us can hope or even wish for. But one should not underrate the power of such works of the imagination. Their mythic images and symbols take up their lodging in our very souls and populate the inner world of our dreams. In the vast majority of cases, they are stronger than the personalities they invade and indoctrinate. The medieval Christian who lived his life enveloped in the tales, songs, poetry, and visual images of the Christian faith could not be anything but a Christian. Nor could the medieval Muslim be anything but a Muslim. The one was as convinced of a heaven of saints and singing angels as the other was of a Paradise garden filled with nubile virgins. Each was quite ready to risk his life fighting the other.

A few centuries after Dante, Ignatius of Loyola (1491–1556), founder of the Society of Jesus, developed a sophisticated method of active imagination that served exactly this purpose of indoctrination. His *Spiritual Exercises* were intended as the bedrock of Jesuit education, especially for those joining the order, but also in modified versions for children and laypeople.[10] The core of the *Exercises* was the imagination of episodes from the Gospels, to be evoked inwardly with as much reality and detail as possible. Not only the inner senses but the emotions were to be aroused, so that the sufferings of Jesus, the joys and sorrows of Mary, etc., would become those of the beholder.

The Jesuits' confidence in the formative effect of the imagination led them also to become pioneers in the arts of the theater and of theatrical architecture,[11] which while they charmed and entertained, stamped the desired images on the inner senses and the soul. It is no wonder that it was a Jesuit, Athanasius Kircher (1602–80), who pioneered the magic lantern and described the first moving light images.[12] What he could have done with the cinema!

In the eighteenth century there occurred one of the most phenomenal irruptions into the world of the imagination: that of Emanuel Swedenborg (1688–1772), an immensely distinguished scientist and statesman.[13] In his younger days, Swedenborg had studied Kabbalistic practices in the London Jewish community and penetrated some of their secrets of breath control and sexual yoga, as we might call it.[14] This laid the groundwork for his breakthrough in 1744, at the age of fifty-six, into the heavens and hells of the universe. He spent the rest of his long life writing theological treatises based on his visions. His endless chronicles of conversations with spirits are often comic—and he was well aware of this; yet there is never any suggestion that the experience was imaginary or merely symbolic.[15] Swedenborg humbly accepted his role as bearer of a new revelation from God to mankind and as the institutor of a New Church for a new age.

What else can a visionary do, once he has given himself, heart and soul, to the power of the imagination? He cannot suspect that the heavenly world revealed to him with such palpable reality might not be the genuine article.

The early nineteenth century saw a further development in the exploration of the imaginal world. It was discovered by the followers of Anton Mesmer (1734–1815) that people, usually women, who had been put into a hypnotic trance could sometimes describe places not of this earth, and answer questions about things they never knew in the waking state. Some, like Swedenborg and Dante, could converse with departed spirits, and hence describe the world that supposedly awaits us all after death. No matter that the "spirits" were often detected in absurdities and lies (as Swedenborg had already noticed), or that the various accounts of other worlds were contradictory: the mediums told what their listeners were eager to hear.

The great question about what is experienced in active imagination concerns its objectivity. The Sufis of Persia, Suhrawardi chief among them, asserted that the world of *Hūrqalyā* that they accessed inwardly was indeed an objective world, but without a material substratum. Consequently others following the same practice would find themselves in the same places, as surely as two travelers to Baghdad would agree that they had visited the same city. The same principle applies to Kabbalistic practice, though there the experiences tend to be more mathematically abstract.

One possibility is that these philosopher-mystics have actually found their way out of Plato's Cave, into the Real World (see chapter 5). In Platonic philosophy this is definitely an objective world, more real than the material one. But how do we explain the striking differences in what is found there, depending on the philosopher's religion?

While Plato's philosopher would meet the Greek gods, the Sufi meets angels and "ascended masters."[16] The Kabbalist may explore, organ by organ and hair by hair, the macrocosmic body of his God.[17] Christians like Dante and Swedenborg are likely to see hell as well as heaven, and so on. The differences are enough to make the modern, agnostic nonvoyager quite skeptical about the objectivity of the Other World.

It is as though each religion, and even each sect, is a kind of exclusive club entered at birth. From childhood onwards, the minds of the members are filled with a certain set of images and symbols that structure their imaginative world, their philosophy, and their expectations for an afterlife. The medieval cathedrals and churches were repositories of such images and symbols, and were tools of indoctrination in the best sense; for when there is imaginal consensus in a society, discord is reduced to a minimum. When those rare persons who were gifted and trained for esoteric practices embarked on their meditations, it was within the same consensus. They saw, heard, felt, and smelt an environment that may have been novel and full of wonders and surprises, but was still controlled by their faith and expectations. Only when the mystic passed beyond the inner senses was he or she liberated from what had been learned through the outer ones. Then, as all readers of mystical reports know, the descriptions become halting: the mystic cannot find words for the experience. It is all light and unity, and paradoxical categories where the rational mind has no foothold.

Since most of us (and I emphatically include myself) are not expert in traveling the inner world of the imagination, we hang the walls of our memory palaces with pictures that others have given us. If we are fortunate, our parents began the process by telling us stories and giving us picture books that filled our imaginations with archetypal images of talking beasts, heroes and heroines, far-off places, comedy and tragedy. Maybe they also brought us up in one of the richly imagistic religious traditions.[18] We may have left its dogmas behind as we grew up, but its mythology is a trust fund on which we will never cease to draw.

If we were unfortunate, our parents parked us in front of the television.[19] And that is the measure of the gulf between the imaginal world of the poor, ignorant medieval peasants and that of today.

CHAPTER

11

The Pagan Renaissance[1]

y the end of the thirteenth century, the Christianization of Europe was complete.[2] Gothic cathedrals and churches radiated their influence over every community, great and small. Mendicant orders like the Franciscans not only preached the Gospel but lived it out, sharing the poverty of their humblest listeners. The universities were flourishing, with an idealized curriculum of the Seven Liberal Arts,[3] crowned by Theology. The cults of saints and their relics, with pilgrimages to their shrines, provided endless variety and interest, and a feeling for the spirits of place. A growing devotion to the Virgin Mary offered a feminine focus for love and prayer that was otherwise wanting in monotheism. Heretics, dissenters, and revanchist pagans were mercilessly suppressed. Few people in Europe could have had any doubt about the existence of heaven, purgatory, and hell, and of what it took to end up in each.

In the ancient past, comparable systems of belief and social control have lasted for thousands of years, as witness the civilizations of China, Egypt, Peru, and the Europe of the megalith builders. In all known instances, the hierarchy was headed by a sacred king, served by the members of an elite administrative order. These possessed scientific and cosmological knowledge that they incorporated in stone monuments and no doubt in other, more ephemeral forms. The life of the masses was structured by religious rituals and obligations, shading off insensibly to secular law and order.[4]

Some people think that the Middle Ages were like that, achieving an equilibrium between the church's spiritual authority and the temporal power that belonged, in theory, to the Holy Roman Emperor. But this seems to me a romantic dream. Unlike the ancient theocracies, the edifice was scarcely in place when cracks began to appear in its fabric. Of course there are individuals who can be blamed for the self-destruction of the ideal Christian civilization.[5] But in retrospect it seems to be impossible to realize eternal values in an age which some call by the Hindu term Kali Yuga or, after the Greek cyclical scheme, the Age of Iron.[6] Nothing seems to last for very long.

The fourteenth century began its sorry tale of decadence with the brutal dissolution of the Order of Knights Templar, and ended it with two rival popes. Soon would come the final schism between the Catholic and Orthodox Churches,[7] then the Reformation and Counter-Reformation, the Wars of Religion, the so-called Enlightenment, and the dismal, soulless state known as modernity.[8] But that story is not our concern. We are trying to trace the influence of those who have always had at heart the spiritual state of our civilization, and we will not find them on one side or the other of these squabbles.

Images, symbols, myths, and archetypes are what truly stamps a culture, rather than theology and faith in things unseen. In the Middle Ages, these coincided; in the Renaissance, they drew apart, as the fifteenth and sixteenth centuries saw a change of revolutionary dimensions in the European imagination. The Christian images did not vanish, but they were joined by a rival body of images, reborn from Greco-Roman antiquity, with which they lived in grudging compromise.

Once in late medieval Siena, a Roman statue of Venus was unearthed. This was in 1345, at a time when the nude was never used gratuitously in art, but only when realism demanded it, as in depictions of Adam and Eve. The newly found example of the classical canon of beauty was mounted on a pedestal in the piazza and admired by the populace. But the two years that followed were full of catastrophe for the city. Fearing that their idolatry had offended God and the Virgin, the pious Sienese took down their Venus, smashed her into little pieces, and buried the remains.[9] This instructive tale illustrates the ambiguous nature of images from the pagan world: they were tremendously attractive, but they carried a whiff of sulfur about them. There was a strong theological tradition that the pagan gods were none other than the fallen demons of Satan's band, who had amused themselves before the coming of Christ by devising false religions for the snaring of mankind.

In the following century the danger was forgotten. Adulation of antiquity was rampant, and the Greco-Roman models were eagerly emulated by sculptors, painters, architects, poets, playwrights, and philosophers. These artists did not cease to turn out works on sacred subjects, as anyone knows who has wearied at the endless Virgins and Children in Italian art museums. But a growing fashion in secular life, starting with the decorative arts and spreading to sculpture and architecture, favored classical subjects. Soon these became the norm, going hand in hand with the education in Latin and Greek favored by the humanists. The homes of the aristocracy were soon adorned with the iconography of Ovid's *Metamorphoses* and Virgil's *Aeneid*, with pagan gods and goddesses, and, not insignificantly, with nude figures.

Imagine the difference between spending the impressionable years of childhood looking at church iconography and Books of Hours, and growing up among walls painted with the loves of Jupiter and the Labors of Hercules! It did not matter that the classical myths were well known to be pure fiction, and their divinities regarded at best as allegorical: the images were powerful and memorable. One reason is that for the first time in many centuries, eroticism had become an acceptable subject for the visual arts. It would remain so right through the prudish nineteenth century, when classical subjects served as the pretext for artists to continue undisturbed with their favorite exercise of depicting sensuous, nude bodies.

Although the Christian and the pagan imaginations cohabited in artists' ateliers, destined respectively for sacred and secular use, their incompatibility must have been felt by the users. Mostly battened down in the unconscious mind, it erupted in religious zeal, bigotry, and conflict, as though one's true beliefs had to be protected at all costs. And indeed, Christian values were under fire, for few (least of all the Renaissance popes and cardinals) would willingly choose the ascetic, self-denying ethos of the Gospels over the colorful, heroic virtues of Hercules, Aeneas, and the historical Romans.

So much for the exoteric effects of the new gods. In the esoteric field, they had an equally revolutionary effect. Chapter 1 mentioned Georgios Gemistos Plethon, the envoy from Mistra to the Council of Florence in 1438–39, and his notion of an Ancient Theology taught by a chain of pre-Christian initiates. Among Plethon's gifts to the Florentines was the singing of Orphic hymns to the classical divinities.[10] Plethon thereby planted the seed which Marsilio Ficino, translator of the works of Plato, Plotinus, and Hermes Trismegistus, cultivated, with spectacular effect on the European magical tradition.[11]

Ficino's magic[12] was grafted on to an existing tradition of medieval magic, which in turn had derived from Arabic sources such as the notorious manual of spirit evocation called *Picatrix*.[13] The fundamental idea was the doctrine of correspondences, which teaches that everything in the universe corresponds to other things on higher or lower levels of being. Thus, for example, the human body corresponds to the Zodiac, whose twelve constellations rule its twelve principal members or organs. The seven planets have their correspondences in the mineral realm as seven metals, while in the vegetable realm they rule various herbs, and so forth. The principle of natural magic is that manipulating something on one level attracts influences from the corresponding thing on another level. So, in a simple example, to wear a golden ring attracts the lordly qualities of the Sun, while a copper bracelet draws the friendly influences of Venus.[14]

The Arabic sources also spoke of magic worked through conscious agents, either angels or demons, whose ranks are arranged according to the laws of correspondence and who can be commanded by the proper rituals.[15] But the dangers of trafficking with demons (who might even impersonate angels) made this a risky activity for Christians and Moslems alike.

The influx of ancient Greek philosophical and wisdom literature greatly expanded these horizons. To Ficino, who was anything but a naïve dabbler, the Hermetic treatises and the writings of Plotinus clarified many things that had been obscure, such as the mechanism by which natural magic works. Once again, the key was the imagination. The imaginative energy was what opened the connection between one level and another, and the more strongly it acted, the most certain were the results. The fuel by which it worked was Eros (love or desire), and the substance on which it imprinted itself was the *spiritus*, or subtle spirit that interpenetrates the material universe.

Based on these principles, Ficino developed a kind of planetary magic in which the magus would surround himself with colors, scents, substances, and music of the kind corresponding to the planet whose influences he wished to attract. These would both draw the influences through their own correspondences and aid him in the intense concentration of his will and imagination. It was a moot point among Renaissance magicians whether the planet was conceived as a purely natural object or as an ensouled being—presumably an angel.

The argument could be raised of why, if one's desire is licit, one shouldn't simply pray to God or the saints for it.

To perform a magical operation instead seems, to conservative believers, to insult the efficacy of prayer and God's wisdom in granting or refusing it. The magician may retort that magic is simply an operation in the natural world, working with specialized knowledge of God's creation and hence no more impious than agriculture. After all, farmers don't follow Christ's injunction to "take no thought for the morrow" (Matt. 6:34), but rely on their knowledge of Nature's laws and act accordingly. Even if the magic involves a spirit or an angel, is this any worse than the commonplace prayer to a saint?

As in the case of the medieval synthesis, the new, pagan imagination of the Renaissance worked on two levels, exoteric and esoteric. In the public domain there were the new palaces and gardens, paintings, sculptures, decorative objects, prints, and books, which were the antithesis of the Gothic cathedrals and of Medieval Christian art. No one could evade the influence of the new imaginal environment, and few would want to, for it opened the senses to the Eros of earthly beauty. All unknowingly, Europeans were becoming Platonists: for while mainstream Christianity spurned natural beauty and erotic attraction, Plato's philosophy embraced them, as the first sprouting of the wings on which the soul would eventually rise to the knowledge of intellectual beauty.[16]

In the more esoteric circles of the highly educated humanists, it was equally impossible to evade the seduction of classical philosophy and the challenge it posed to the Christian view of the world. As we have seen in chapter 1, Plethon's lineage of pagan sages opened up a vision of the distant past in which all God's peoples were endowed with a wisdom appropriate to their time and place. The newly discovered texts of Hermes, Zoroaster, Plato, etc., set a thorny problem to those obliged to reconcile them with the Christian revelation.

The inhabitants of old European cities still live their lives among the evidence of this split imagination: the Gothic cathedral and churches on the one hand, the Renaissance palaces on the other, with their contrary iconographies. It is a rich, even overrich combination, mixing two worldviews that, for all the well-meaning efforts of synthesis, remain an unsolved conundrum in the history of consciousness. Moses and Homer; Caesar and Christ: whether we like them or not, these are the twin roots of our spiritual heritage.

CHAPTER

12

The Philosopher's Dilemma

*I*n every generation there have been a few people who did not believe so much as *know* some of the answers to the eternal questions of humanity.[1] Their knowledge is notoriously difficult to convey to the rest of us, but its radiance and certainty act as a beacon and a reminder of what a man or woman may be. In an ordered and traditional society, there is a place for them: like Catherine of Siena or Nicholas of Cusa,[2] they command the respect of kings and popes, and set a standard of holiness and wisdom to which the clergy (if not insanely jealous) aspire. But what do they do when the spiritual equilibrium of the world falls apart, as it did during the fifteenth century with the East-West schism and the influx of humanism; in the sixteenth, with the Reformation, Counter-Reformation, and Wars of Religion; and in the seventeenth, with the witchcraft mania, the Thirty Years' War, and the scientific revolution?

The evidence points in two directions. Some of the Wise made efforts behind the scenes toward the healing and renovation of society. Others worked to bring illumination to individuals. The first are visible in Rosicrucianism at the beginning of the seventeenth century; the second, who will be treated in the next chapter, in alchemy and theosophy.

The philosopher's dilemma is the choice between these two fields of action, the political and the personal. It may be phrased thus: Can the state of humanity as a whole be remedied, or is it in such a parlous case that remedy is only possible on the individual level?

One does not have to be excessively wise to be troubled by this question, but to answer it requires a sounding of one's deepest convictions about human nature and the place of man on earth. For example, does one believe that life on earth is merely a prelude to a much more important life that begins after death? If so, the social conditions of this vale of tears are a secondary matter, even a distraction. Does one believe, with most Christians, that everyone has an individual and immortal soul, or, with some pagans, that personal immortality is won only by titanic efforts? Is there a clear distinction between material and spiritual existence, or are body and soul both part of a continuum that is split by our misperception? Should I concern myself with humanity as a whole, or with my own salvation, leaving the rest to Divine Providence or the goddess Fortuna? Am I a separate unit with my own spiritual history, a stranger or even exile on this earth (the Gnostic point of view), or do I belong to a tribe, race, or species with a macrohistory of past and future evolution?

In the sixteenth century there were three main doctrinal streams in Europe whose business it was to spare people the trouble that such questions cause. Catholics were advised to leave weighty theological matters to the Church, as agent of God's will on earth, and to try to live a virtuous life according to her teachings. Martin Luther, on the contrary, held that everyone had a right to seek his or her own answers, but that God had placed these unerringly in the Scriptures. The sectaries of John Calvin neatly divided humanity into predestined groups of the saved and the damned, and hoped that their conduct and fortunes proved them to be among the former. By the middle of the century all three factions were at daggers drawn, while the Jews, patiently awaiting their Messiah, did their best to keep out of the crossfire.[3]

It will always be a mystery how the religion whose primary commandments are love of God, and love of others, came to such a pass. But a clue must lie in some of the beliefs that were grafted onto the stem of the Gospels. What educated Stoic or Platonist could ever have taken literally the doctrines of predestination and transubstantiation, the infallibility of the Scriptures, or the purchase of indulgences to shorten one's time in purgatory? What thoughtful Christian could avoid creeping doubts about such things? The axiom that those who feel insecure in their own beliefs often react with aggressive dogmatism was amply demonstrated.

The first grand and sweeping solution to the philosopher's dilemma was that of Ignatius of Loyola, already mentioned in chapter 10. The Jesuits' method took the bull by both horns. On the personal level, it trained its members through the use of the active imagination to become single-minded warriors for Christ and the Catholic faith. At the end of the *Spiritual Exercises* there is no room for doubt: what the novice was taught to believe, he now *knows*, and an unshakable faith renders him ready even for martyrdom.

On the collective level, the Jesuits' intention was to convert the entire world to the Catholic faith. Being more intelligent than some other monastic orders, they realized that this was better done by stealth than by the bludgeon and the stake. Jesuit education therefore celebrated the glory and variety of the God-created world. It built on the natural curiosity of the young, encouraged theatrics (a branch of the imagination) and the applied sciences. In times of religious stalemate, even Protestants would send their children to Jesuit schools.[4] Ignatius's missionaries, who formed the first global organization, learned the languages and religions of their hosts, then adjusted their conversion strategies accordingly. Sometimes they almost "went native" in the course of their infiltration, and sent home reports that are a priceless source for historical ethnography. But always there was the adamantine will to bring about one, and only one end; and this was used, say the Jesuits' critics, to justify dubious and sinister means. Also one wonders whether there is any validity in the "knowledge" attained through the *Spiritual Exercises*, or whether it is a fanatical reinforcement of prescribed answers to the eternal questions.

There is little comparison between the powerful Jesuit order and the homemade concoctions of a few Lutheran friends that launched the Rosicrucian movement in the second decade of the seventeenth century.[5] But the two tracts, the *Fame* and the *Confession* of the Brethren of the Rosy

Cross, fell on the fertile ground of a Europe avid for a spiritual food above and beyond what the churches had to offer. Thus a new myth was created of a secret fraternity of wise initiates who genuinely wish the best for humanity and toil behind the scenes to bring it about. Many people were, and still are, aching to believe this.

The Rosicrucian manifestos circulated in manuscript from 1611, then appeared in print in 1614 and 1615, followed in 1616 by their pendant, the fantasy novel *The Chemical Wedding of Christian Rosenkreuz*. The manifestos played on the mythic themes of a traveler who brings to Europe the secret teachings of the East; the burial of his body and his wisdom, and the opening of his vault 120 years later; the foundation of a fraternity of wise men who move incognito among the nations, healing the body in their capacity as physicians, and working to heal the soul of Europe; and the announcement that the time has now come for rebirth.

The Rosicrucian writings come out of a Lutheran milieu influenced by the Hermetic physician Paracelsus (1493–1541) and by alchemy. They claim that the Brethren draw their wisdom from twin sources: the Bible and the Book of Nature, and they urge the world to do likewise. There is no room for the Catholic hierarchy, and no emphasis on damnation. The *Chemical Wedding* blends Christian theosophy with a cult of Venus as goddess of Nature and patron of alchemy.[6] It is strongly influenced by that epic of the pagan revival, the *Hypnerotomachia Poliphili* of Francesco Colonna.[7]

The Rosicrucian enterprise belongs to the movement known as Pansophy (literally "all-wisdom"), which combines the natural with the supernatural sciences for the betterment of the world. One founder of the pansophic current was John Dee (1527–1609), who had urged English artisans to study mathematics for the better mastery of technology, then had pursued his own research through "angelic conversations."[8] Another was Paracelsus, whose conception of a living Nature, shot through by celestial influences and responsive to alchemy, was combined with a solid knowledge of herbalism, of chemistry, and of the Scriptures.[9] A fertile breeding-ground of Pansophy was Prague, where Emperor Rudolf II (reigned 1576–1611) allowed as much religious diversity as conditions would permit, and encouraged every art and science, especially the Hermetic ones.[10]

The genius of the Rosicrucian group, whether intentional or not, was to hit on the ingredients for a lasting myth. The final paroxysm of the Wars of Religion, the Thirty Years' War (1618–48), interrupted but did not extinguish it. In Protestant lands, the Rosicrucians could pass as a kind of counter-Jesuit order: noncoercive, nondogmatic, and open to the occult potentials which so scared the churches. But Pansophy now also became counterscientific, in the sense of offering an alternative to an increasingly positivist and materialistic science.

A good illustration of the philosopher's dilemma is the career of the Englishman Elias Ashmole (1617–1692).[11] He was interested from a young age in the occult sciences, especially astrology, and started out as a promising lawyer and public servant. But since he served King Charles I, who was deposed and beheaded in 1649, he had to spend the Commonwealth era in obscurity. For fifteen years he made a deep study of the natural sciences, especially alchemy, medicine, and botany; and of antiquarian matters: heraldry, genealogy, numismatics, and the history of knightly orders. With the Restoration of Charles II in 1660, Ashmole was ready for public service again, and became a kind of master of ceremonies for the monarchy. He wrote a great history of the Order of the Garter, stage-managed its rites (which often involved foreign potentates), and served as authority on all matters of tradition and precedence.

Ashmole was like some chief Druid or Pontifex Maximus, born out of time—and all the more so since every decision he took was governed by horary astrology. His work was a monument to the traditional, hierarchical concept of an orderly society ruled by an anointed King. But far from being insular, he was also a voracious collector of antiquarian objects and of curiosities, natural and artificial, from all over the world. Like the Jesuit Athanasius Kircher, whose ethnographic collection was built on the contributions of missionaries, Ashmole was a founder of one of the earliest museums. He was also a founding member of the Royal Society. In accordance with the pansophic ideal of universal education, he gave his collections to Oxford University, to be open to the public as the Ashmolean Museum.

Wise men such as Ashmole are not necessarily pious or saintly people, nor do they always share current moral and egalitarian ideals. It is not a question of who is right or wrong: they do what they have to do, because they see more clearly and more deeply than the rest of us. And perhaps they serve other gods than ours.

A new Rosicrucian order appeared in the eighteenth century. It was first described in 1710 by "Sincerus Renatus" (a Silesian minister, Samuel Richter) and institutionalized around mid-century. Unlike the original, this "Order of the Golden and Rosy Cross" (Gold- und Rosenkreutz) was fairly visible, and some of its members, headed by King Frederick William II of Prussia, wielded real power.[12] Like other "enlightened despots" of their time,[13] they approved of religious freedom and some civil liberties for the masses. For themselves, the order provided an elaborate system of rituals, grades, titles, and symbols by which they climbed the ladder of initiation. There was much interest in alchemy, and even some kind of magical evocation.

The new Rosicrucianism dropped the polemic against the pope and his church that had marked the original *Confession*, and in the spirit of the new century opened its doors to Catholics as well as to Protestants of various denominations. By steering between the twin shallows of sectarian religion and scientism, it evaded the rivalry between the two that, in the historians' limited picture, characterized the Age of Enlightenment.

The Golden and Rosy Cross was closely connected to the more hierarchical and ceremonial wing of Freemasonry, whose history also illustrates our theme. Elias Ashmole, as it happens, is the first known person to have been initiated into a lodge of Masons as a nonoperative member. That was in 1646. It is not difficult to see why he was drawn to it. Legend has it, and recent scholarship tends to confirm,[14] that after the Order of Knights Templar was suppressed in 1307, some knights escaped to Scotland and kept the Templar tradition secretly alive there. Naturally they had to cease from the public work that had made them the first international bankers and the ensurers of safe passage for pilgrims to the Holy Land. An understandable affinity drew them into alliance with the Scottish guild of masons or architects, whose craft mythology referred to the most famous of all ancient buildings, the Temple of Solomon. Apocryphal legends about the temple and its builders served the guild for initiation rites and as a source of moralizing allegory. For instance, the human being was likened to a raw, unshaped stone fresh from the quarry, which must be chipped, shaped, and polished in order to be worthy of taking its place in the finished building. Society is, by implication, a temple in the making, where God will eventually dwell.

In traditional Freemasonry, the three initiations of Apprentice, Fellow Craft, and Master are quasi-sacramental rites that bring about a transformation in the person. They work not with allegory (which is merely giving things different names) but with symbolism. A symbol does not have just one meaning, like the Statue of Liberty: it has multiple meanings and serves as a link between levels of reality. For example, the black and white squares of the checkerboard floor used in some Masonic lodges do not stand only for the mixture of good and evil in the world, but for the two complementary forces out of which the cosmos is made. These manifest as expansion and contraction, day and night, male and female, and a hundred other pairs. To realize this is to gain an understanding of one way in which the "Great Architect of the Universe" works, from the top to the bottom of his creation. It also conceals a profound teaching about good and evil.[15]

Alongside the initiatic and hierarchical orders, a contrary sort of Freemasonry developed in tune with the currents of secularism, progress, optimism, and egalitarianism.

To this way of thinking, which had its unacknowledged roots in the Gospels, the obstacles to universal brotherhood were a church which still wanted to hang on to its worldly power, and absolute monarchy. Because of their privacy, secrecy, and wide network, some Masonic lodges served as hotbeds of freethinking, and, later in the century, of revolution.[16] For this reason they were periodically closed down and banned by law, as were the Jesuits. Both movements represented a menace that could not be tolerated by those trying to hold society in fragile equilibrium.[17]

By the early nineteenth century, the socially progressive wing of Freemasonry had supplanted the initiatic and hierarchical one, which spawned a variety of magical and fringe-Masonic Orders. Consequently, Rosicrucianism and Freemasonry today have virtually exchanged their original positions. Whereas the Rosicrucianism of 1614 wanted to renovate the world, the modern groups sailing under its banner have no social effect,[18] but provide individuals with teachings and practices for self-improvement through occultism. Whereas the earliest Freemasonry was chivalric and initiatic, now it is secularized and philanthropic, with no view of personal transformation beyond the ethical level. In the United States its influence is diluted among many other fraternal orders with even less traditional content. In short, the philosophers who, according to Plato, should have been compelled to be our rulers, or at least to be the power behind the throne, have packed their bags and left.[19]

Inner Alchemy

onsidering the mystical reports of Protestant and Catholic mystics, Kabbalists and Sufis, it is a truism that their experiences tend to converge in a sense of self-identification with the divine, and in an inexpressible certainty beyond words and images. But down here, there is no guarantee that the "Divine Will" is one and the same for all people and all times. It seems much more likely that it rejoices in variety and, dare one say, in conflict. For there is nothing like conflict for focusing one's intentions and strengthening one's resolve. The sages may meet in sublime concord in the courts of heaven, but they are anything but uniform in their earthly personalities. Nor do they seem to be in the habit of clustering together, almost as though it would be a waste of effort for them to do so. They are more like great, isolated trees of different species, each providing shelter and homes for innumerable lesser creatures, and seeds that may or may not attain the same grandeur.

One such tree is Jacob Boehme (1575–1624), the shoemaker of Görlitz, Silesia (in today's Poland) who forms the historical nexus between the Rhineland mystics (Meister Eckhart, Suso, Tauler, etc.) and the theosophers of the seventeenth, eighteenth, and nineteenth centuries. Boehme's writings are almost unreadable today, but the simple fact of his being shone like a beacon through the dark ages of secular "enlightenment." Here was an artisan and a family man—not a pastor or monk, cardinal or aristocrat—who was chosen for the unveiling of the most profound mysteries, and who lived not in the simple faith befitting his station, but in the vivid consciousness of God. Boehme's example showed that Christianity could be more than ethics and the Scriptures (though he was quite expert in these); more than rites, aestheticism, and sacraments. It could be an inner reality more real than anything in the world and more precious than anything the world could teach. As he says of his first great experience of 1600, "in that quarter hour I saw and learnt more than if I had studied many years in some university . . . for I perceived and recognized the Being of all beings."

What most differentiates Christian theosophy[1] from the mainly Catholic tradition of mysticism is that, as an experiential path, it addresses the intellect as well as the emotions. It does not lack the emotional side and even its own spiritual eroticism, but it also penetrates the workings of metaphysics and cosmology. It may be unnecessary to know how the parts of the human soul and spirit function, or what the different hierarchies of angels are up to, or how

complicated God's own being is. But some people are inquis-
itive by nature, and are not content to be told to mind their
own business and leave these matters to those who understand them. "I do understand them," is Boehme's message,
"because I have seen, felt, and been them." If this is what man
is capable of, why not use our divine gift of understanding
rather than crouching in ignorance disguised as humility?

Theosophy takes the Protestant principle to its highest
conclusion. The "priesthood of every believer" and the right
to search the Scriptures are raised from sermonizing and
bible-study to earth-shattering experiences and illumina-
tions. Nor are there lacking Catholic theosophers, such as
Louis-Claude de Saint-Martin (1743–1802) or Franz von
Baader (1765–1841),[2] equally tired of the complacency
and dullness into which their religion had sunk, who took
Boehme as their master.

The intellectual side of theosophy is more than the
mere satisfaction of curiosity: it is a gnosis, that is to say the
conscious integration of the human subject with its own
transcendent nature. True to the Hermetic principle "as
above, so below," Boehme's discovery of God is also a discovery of himself as a divine being. His God is an agonizing
and dynamic process in which the Unmanifest makes itself
known to itself. The seven qualities engendered by this
process give rise to all the variety of the cosmos, and to its
cyclical and equally agonistic evolution. Consequently, the
contradictions and conflicts of which we are well aware have
their roots not merely in Lucifer's rebellion and in the Fall
of Man, but in the very being of God. We are participants
in the process as individuals, as the human race, and as
Nature. "Yea, God is so near thee, that the birth of the Holy

Trinity is done or wrought even in thy heart, yea, all the three Persons are generated in thy heart, even God the Father, Son, and Holy Ghost."[3] As Jane Leade, a posthumous disciple of Boehme, put it, "Thus shall each one become a Christ (or an Anointed) from this deified root opening within their own soul."

Orthodoxy rightly shuns such dicta because of the damage they can do to weak and suggestible souls. But just as all the sages meet on the mountaintop, they are the place at which, as Boehme was well aware, Christianity and Kabbalah, Hermetism and alchemy all conjoin—to which we can add Sufism, the Hinduism of the Upanishads, and Mahayana Buddhism.

The physicist Basarab Nicolescu has also demonstrated the parallels between Boehme's system and postquantum physics.[4] This seems to me more than coincidence: why shouldn't the spiritual eye have revealed fundamental truths about the nature of things, which materialistic science is just beginning to discover in its clumsier, one-dimensional way? Nicolescu has called loudly and clearly for recognition of the metaphysical values raised by both theosophy and modern physics, for an ethical science, and a new philosophy of Nature.[5] The Nature of the theosophers, ancient and modern, is not an automaton or a blind evolutionary impulse, but a conscious being and, strangely enough, a part of man for which he is responsible.[6]

The principles at play in Boehme's cosmology, as in physics, are few and fixed, and feature simple numbers. But the way they will work themselves out down here is not yet determined; and neither is the fate of this particular human and natural experiment. It is science that has now put the potential tools of destruction and transmutation into the hands of the Luciferically[7] ignorant. Is there any chance to enlighten them, or will this be another failed creation? The aware scientist can hardly be optimistic, but the theosopher knows that whatever the fate of the planet, there is still the chance for the individual to achieve in this life what Boehme calls the "new birth."

The Behmenists of Germany and the Netherlands, France, England and Pennsylvania, are a bright thread of gnosis that runs through the desolate religious landscape of early modern history. Some of them kept largely to themselves, like Saint-Martin, while others formed close-knit circles like that of John Pordage (1607–1681) and Jane Leade (1624–1704) in London. Johann Georg Gichtel (1638–1710) in Amsterdam, who was one of the most creative exegetes of Boehme, gathered a "Society of the Thirty" scattered in various towns. And these were not mere students, but had theosophic experiences of their own that served as confirmation of Boehme's principles. On the fringes of the Behmenists was the quasi-monastic community of Conrad Beissel (1690–1768), who came to the New World in 1720 and whose beautiful, austere buildings still stand in Ephrata, Pennsylvania.[8]

In principle, the way of the Christian theosophist is a strictly inward path, and no one else need know about it. There is no telling how many sincere souls have trodden it, with or without the help of Jacob Boehme. But it is questionable how far the other topic of this chapter, alchemy, is also an inward path.

In many respects alchemy and theosophy are parallel, if not identical in intention, but their imaginal vocabulary is different. Christian theosophy expects, and receives, experiences in the imaginal world that clothe themselves in Biblical figures and symbols: the Trinity, Lucifer, Christ, the Virgin Sophia, etc. The *dramatis personae* of alchemy consist rather of metals and minerals (Mercury, sulphur, salt, magnesia, antimony, silver, gold, etc.), a menagerie of animals and birds (dragon, lion, toad, eagle, pelican, peacock, etc.), and a number of figures from classical mythology (the seven planetary gods and goddesses, plus Hercules, Atalanta, Osiris, etc.). Certainly there have been Christian (and Jewish, and Islamic) overlays to alchemy, just as there is an alchemical overlay to Boehme's theosophy, but its principles and goals were established independently of Moses and before Christ.[9]

The literature of alchemy purports to give instructions for laboratory work with physical substances, and the first level of interpretation of its symbols is as a prescientific code for chemical procedures. Historians of science have shown that alchemical texts do give workable instructions, e.g., for the extraction of gold from compounds by means of antimony.

But especially from 1600, coinciding with Behmenist theosophy and kindred movements, alchemical texts seem to have become less and less chemical. Writers like Heinrich Khunrath, Cesare della Riviera, and Thomas Vaughan[10] were clearly interested less in laboratory work than in a spiritual form of alchemy.

The principle of spiritual alchemy is that the substances represent elements in man and the spiritual world, and the procedures take place within his soul. To give some simple examples, the alembic or crucible is the human psychophysical complex, and the laboratory is the *mundus imaginalis,* the real but nonphysical universe in which spiritual transmutations take place. The "fire" is the deliberate inner effort of meditation (incidentally inducing a feeling of heat); its regulation by "bellows" is done by control of the breath, as in yoga. The purification of the material already requires a more than common control over the mind (the "fixation of Mercury"), but only then does the real work of transmutation occur. There is a real danger of the vessel exploding—presumably in physical or nervous breakdown. At every stage the operator meets with opposing forces which must be dominated, or else he must go back and try again. As in Boehme's cosmos, these forces are real beings who try to keep him from his goal, yet at the same time they are part of himself. It requires heroic efforts and the conquest of multiple fears in order to keep one's "matter" intact throughout the work, i.e., to persist in this inner quest, which brings the seeker into situations absolutely unimaginable to the outsider.[11] The gold that rests in the crucible at the end is the utterly transformed Self of the hero who has fought the battle and won. It is also the Universal Panacea, because it is the cure for all the ills of mortality. For one in whose heart (to quote Boehme) "the Holy Trinity is wrought," death can be no more than an accident of chemistry.[12]

It was C.G. Jung who revalidated alchemy for the educated public, rescuing it from becoming a footnote to the history of chemistry.[13] In a series of masterful books, he showed how laboratory processes which make no sense in modern chemical terms could have symbolized processes in the alchemist's psyche or soul. The old alchemists, in this view, either did not know that their chemical efforts were really bringing about a personal transformation, or else they deliberately couched their psychological and spiritual experiences in chemical allegories. However, Jung's "integration of the personality" hardly seems to match the heaven-storming goal described above—though it might be a wise prerequisite.

Simultaneously with the propagation of Jung's theory of alchemy, there came a protest against his too-inward tendency, his psychologizing of this discipline. The writings of the mysterious Fulcanelli[14] were at the origin of this. Nothing certain is known of this reputed adept, least of all his real identity, but thanks to his writings, France became the center of a new interest in operative alchemy.

After World War II, Frater Albertus (Albert Riedel) and Jean Dubuis, founder of the Philosophers of Nature, broke the centuries-old habits of obscurantism and secrecy (from which even Fulcanelli cannot be excused), and taught alchemical processes in modern labs.[15] The goal of transmuting base metals into gold, whether understood spiritually or physically, was set aside in favor of more attainable goals, especially the making of medicines through "spagyric" processes, i.e., the separation of the subtle elements of plants and minerals.[16] The new alchemists work with physical substances, but with an awareness of subtle forces (planetary, elemental, even angelic), and of the operator's effect on the material. Conversely, the spagyrical process is reflected, Jungian fashion, in the operator's soul.

The scientific principle of the universal repeatability of an experiment is meaningless in practical alchemy: things will not work if one lacks the requisite "virtue." There is not even any hard-and-fast division between the physical and the psychic, so intimately are they linked by the principle of correspondence. An attitude of reverence toward Nature is paramount. If there is a vanguard of the future science—the only kind that we can afford to sustain—it is here.

The proponents of the different kinds of alchemy are different psychological types, and as such are unlikely to favor each other's methods. Those who work with physical substances do so because it suits them, but it is just as well that the process of human transmutation can go forward without the expense of a well-equipped laboratory. Otherwise poor Jacob Boehme would not have got far. However, if we can believe what we read, is it not extraordinary that, when interpreted one way, chemical recipes deriving from Alexandrian Egypt work in the laboratory, and in another way, provide reliable guidance on the theosophic path? How could these two such different fields be connected?

Yes, it is extraordinary to the modern mind, so brilliant in physics and chemistry, so ignorant of the inner and the imaginal world. It is almost touching, this childlike faith that the world of matter is the only real one, and all the rest, epiphenomena of it. But what if we were to turn the tables and suggest that the inner world is prior to the outer?[17] That the imagination precedes rather than follows the event? That the only reason we see the stars is that we share, for that moment, in their perpetual creation? Then it would be the mental and imaginal states that are primary, and the chemical procedures that are secondary to them. As normal, undeveloped people, we are only able to perceive and live in a normal, undeveloped world, which is the world known to science. But once supernormal conscious states had been mastered, then one might live in a supernormal world with different laws from those of classical physics. This, incidentally, would explain the miracles of healing attributed to Christ and others; and even the turning of lead into gold.

The Religion of Art

*I*n the preceding chapters, we have surveyed some of the movements that sought to fill the void left by the demise of Catholic Christianity: Neopaganism, Rosicrucianism, Freemasonry, theosophy, and alchemy. But however authentic the spiritual experiences they offered, none of these movements was completely satisfactory. They were esotericisms without a corresponding exotericism; they served a secretive elite, but did nothing for the masses of ordinary religious people.

Once, men and women of high spiritual attainment and profound esoteric knowledge had worked as leaders in the Church and were revered as saints. There were Pope Sylvester II (Gerbert d'Aurillac, c. 945–1003), architect of the Holy Roman Empire; Abbot Suger, father of the Gothic cathedral; women mystics with practical and political influence like Hildegard of Bingen and Theresa of Avila;

philosophers like Aquinas, Bonaventura, Nicholas of Cusa; saints like Bernard and Francis; and the Order of Knights Templar. But the Catholic Church has lost the dimensions represented by such people, while few of the innumerable Protestant sects ever wanted them.

Lacking the presence of such examples, the very notion of religious experience faded from the mental world of the majority, Christians included. The rational but still church-going eighteenth century gave to the word "enthusiasm" (from the Greek *enthousiasmos*, possession by a god) the pejorative meaning of "ill-regulated religious emotion or specula-tion."[1] The whole idea had become uncomfortable and was shunned in polite conversation.

Cold-shouldered by organized religion, enthusiasm now entered by another doorway: that of the arts. This is the inner meaning of the movement known as Romanticism. The keywords of Romanticism, dutifully learned by adolescents bored to tears by Wordsworth and Shelley, are like so many compass-needles all pointing to a single pole. Subjectivity; Imagination; the sublime; pantheism and the ensoulment of Nature; fantasies of the medieval past. Let us take them one by one.

Subjectivity and interest in one's own inner processes and emotions is the *sine qua non* of the esoteric path. Although it can stop short at a neurotic self-centeredness, it holds the beginning of self-observation and the promise of self-knowledge.

The Imagination, as distinct from mere fantasy, is the primary tool, or weapon, of esoteric work. It is that where-by one discovers a world within, and learns to act in it rather than to be a passive spectator. It gives access, via symbols, to levels of being that are immaterial, but real and even formative with regard to the physical.

The sublime—found in mountains, volcanoes, the ocean, the heavens, night, heroism and tragedy—lifts man out of the everyday and into a cosmic awareness. It gives him the first inkling of his own potential grandeur and divinity, though this may dawn as a feeling of personal nullity.

The certainty that Nature is alive and ensouled acted as a corrective to two errors. One was the Christian mistrust of Nature, which had its doctrinal roots in Christ's "kingdom not of this world," and its practical reason in the need to convert pagan nature-worshipers. Another was the utilitarian attitude of the early Enlightenment, e.g., Descartes' idea that animals are simply machines, or the Deists' concept of a clockwork universe free from the inconvenience of divine intervention. Pantheism holds that Nature *is* God, but this is insufficient for esotericism, which demands a metaphysical dimension beyond what the physical world contains and reveals.

The Romantic fantasies about the medieval past were historically inaccurate and, to a later and cynical eye, rather laughable.[2] But they rested on an intuition of the integrity of the medieval spiritual world, as mentioned above. That was the last time when Europe was whole, sharing a single faith in the undivided Catholic Church, and a single chivalric ethos. It never worked perfectly, but the ideal was there: of an emperor whose authority counted above that of kings and local lords, because it came from God.[3]

Romantic medievalism was also a reaction against Classicism, which had degenerated from the balmy days of the

Italian Renaissance into a stultifying system of education. Generations of small boys had Latin, Greek, and ancient history beaten into them, so that when they grew up and became important men they could impress their peers with quips from Horace and Martial. They knew little, and cared less, for their own national and ethnic traditions: Greco-Roman civilization was their cynosure. Consequently, when Johann Wolfgang von Goethe looked at the Gothic wonder of Strasburg Cathedral in 1770, he *saw* something that had been unseen for centuries.[4] When the Brothers Grimm collected German fairy tales and made their German dictionary, they opened a vein that had been not only dormant but suppressed during the classical hegemony.

A word should be said here about the connection between Romanticism, nationalism, and esotericism. Each nation, if one looks back far enough, has its own mythology, its own flavor of spirituality, and its own sacred traditions which were once reflected in the cycles of daily life. It was these that were rediscovered and revalued by the Romantic movement. However, there were exceptions in the former British colonies (the United States, Canada, Australia, and New Zealand), whose settlers more or less extirpated the traditions of their native peoples, which in any case do not suit Europeans. The colonizers lacked the nourishment of the soul which comes from living on the land of one's forebears, and from daily contact with their legacy: churches, castles, saints' days, processions, festivals, local shrines and legends. The new lands can offer the feeling of the sublime and a certain nature mysticism (best seen in the American Transcendentalists), but they lack the continuity that leads from shared mythology and symbolism, through exoteric religion and ritual, to mysticism and the esoteric way. For better or worse, they must reconstruct the latter according to their own lights.

The primary arts of the Renaissance were visual—painting, sculpture, and architecture. Those of the Romantic era were aural—poetry, imaginative prose, and music. The latter arts act as a more powerful stimulus to the inward path because of the different functions of the eye and the ear. The eye gives us immediate and detailed knowledge of the physical world surrounding us; it draws us out of ourselves, so much so that most people forget that they are even there. The ear also draws us, but not so much out of as into ourselves. We always have to interpret what we hear, because it comes through language rather than with the immediacy of forms and colors. When we read poetry, and even more when we hear it spoken, it causes images to arise from inside, rather than from without. We create and own them in a way that we can never do with the outside world.

The Romantic poets discovered states of the soul that no one had paid attention to before, and then educated generations of readers to feel them. The reason poetry was so effective for this process is because of its fixity with regard to language. The poem is inseparable from its actual words and all the resonances they evoke in native speakers (which is why lyric poetry especially is untranslatable). Also, because of its rhyme and meter, it sticks in the memory in a way that prose does not. Lines such as "They flash upon that inward eye, which is the bliss of solitude" (Wordsworth's "Daffodils") or "He prayeth best, who loveth best all things both great and small" (Coleridge's *Ancient Mariner*) become part of one's very self. Poetic maxims such as Goethe's "Stirb und werde" (Die and become!) or "Das ewig Weibliche zieht uns heran" (The eternal feminine draws us upward) contain an entire philosophy, if not actually a religion.

Since the Muse of poetry today is virtually dormant,[5] let us turn to novels, which are very much a creation of the Romantic era. Here indeed is the back door through which celestial influences entered, to work on a vast sector of society. One might not think of the great nineteenth-century novelists like Dickens, Hugo, and Balzac as "spiritual," but this is to underrate their insights into human nature, their depiction of archetypal figures, and their sense of the dance of destiny and freewill. Less well known are the consciously esoteric novels of Novalis, Hoffmann, Nerval, Nodier, and the once best-sellers of George Sand and Bulwer-Lytton.[6]

The novel reader enters an alternative universe of images, personalities, and events, that can be more real—because more romantic—than our everyday reality. The value of the experience is borne out even today, when, far from having been driven out by the competition of television and cinema, the novel is alive and well. This is probably because it is the one serious art form to have stolidly resisted the alienating influence of modernism.

When we move from literature to music, the transition is potentially as radical as that from the visual to the verbal arts, for music is the most insubstantial of all the arts, and the least indebted to the external world for its material. Only potentially, however, for in many whole cultures, and for the majority of people in our own, music is only a handmaid to poetry. Their music all consists of "songs," in which the music enhances the words if they are present, or suggests them if they are absent. Pure music does not exist for them, because even when they listen to instrumental music, they accompany it themselves with a sequence of thoughts, associations, inner images, and words, and these become the meaning of the work for them.

Composers have always been content with, or at least resigned to, this use of their craft. They know that much of their music will not be heard as such, but will be a background to social or religious functions. (The Muzak industry knows that one does not have to hear music consciously in order to be influenced by it.) But in the Romantic era, for the first time, composers regarded themselves not as craftsmen but as "artists," borrowing a status that had first been accorded to the masters of the Italian Renaissance. This change was achieved above all thanks to Mozart, whose prodigious gift appeared as more than human; and by Beethoven, who fitted perfectly the archetype of the sublimely inspired artist, then, after his deafness, that of the tragic hero.[7] Because it was divinely inspired, their music demanded attention and devotion, not mere consumption like the work of common craftsmen.

The Viennese composers Haydn, Mozart, and Beethoven felt no need for words to accompany their most profound musical utterances. Simultaneously, a group of German writers began to praise absolute music as the very highest of the arts, because it can transport one into another mode of being: a mode in which the meaning is crystal-clear and the feeling palpable, even though there are no words or images that adequately express them. To those able to suppress the verbal and visual associations, absolute music offers something akin to meditational states. It seems to be its own world, with its own inexorable laws, which exists above and prior to our normal state. In other words, it is a form of the *mundus imaginalis*.

The Traditionalists have nothing good to say about the art-religion of Romanticism, which they regard, with good reason, as a competitor, and as a pseudoreligion of aesthetic self-indulgence. If anyone doubts that the art-religion is alive today, they should go to a big art museum on a Sunday and see the people making their devotions. Some are there because they love it; others have made the pilgrimage to better themselves; children are there because it is thought to be good for them, just like church in the old days. But what is missing is the sense of the sacred, to say nothing of a community devoted to its members.

The art-religion whose hierophants were Goethe and Beethoven, Byron and Victor Hugo, reached its culmination in Richard Wagner, composer of *The Ring of the Nibelung, Tristan and Isolde, The Mastersingers of Nuremberg,* and *Parsifal*.[8] Wagner's music dramas purported to be a synthesis of all the arts, and he built a templelike theater for them at Bayreuth (Bavaria), sincerely believing that they might save civilization and rescue Europe from degeneracy. The fact that Wagner's operas still have so many devotees today gives one pause for thought. The musicologist H. C. Robbins Landon once remarked that the *Ring* "becomes more important to humanity every year, its truths more compelling (possibly because *Götterdämmerung* is a closer reality than it ever was before),"[9] The *Ring* is a prophetic work, which, in music of incomparable power and beauty, depicts the coming of evil into an innocent world, the rise of mankind to consciousness, the withdrawal of the gods, and the end of a cosmic cycle. Where is hope in this?

Only in love. And love itself, as Wagner went on to show in *Tristan and Isolde*, finds its consummation not in the fullness of life but in the extinction of the self and in cosmic oblivion. Only in his last opera, *Parsifal*, did he really hold out hope for the future, in the founding of an order under a pure and tested leader. And we seem very far from that today.

The religion of art has its low points, equivalent perhaps to televangelism; a slippery slope leads from the museum's blockbuster show to Disneyland. But the best of Romanticism is more than sensation and aestheticism. It is philosophy in action, energized as Plato believed it should be—through the Eros of beauty.

CHAPTER

15

Wise Men from the East

*T*here is an old tradition that at some time during the seventeenth century, the original Brothers of the Rosy Cross left Europe and went to India, to live a more tranquil life there.[1] I take this as a symbolic statement, meaning that the renovation of the whole world heralded in the Rosicrucian manifestos had failed, and that Western civilization was henceforth abandoned to its own devices. The mention of India, however, is curious. Who at the time would have thought of that land as a suitable home for wise men? During the following century, while the Indian subcontinent was being colonized, it passed in the Western imagination for a pit of ignorance and superstition, of untouchables, holy cows, and wife-burning. Yet ironically enough, the next appearance of a spiritual mission to Europe (and, by then, also to America) came precisely from there.

It was the Theosophical Society, founded in 1875, that first propagated Eastern philosophy in the West, not just as a subject of scholarly or cultural interest, but as the foundation for spiritual renewal. The society's prime mover, Helena P. Blavatsky (1831–1891), saw Europe and America as mired in two incompatible and equally false faiths: that of dogmatic, exoteric Christianity, and that of materialistic science.[2] After an attempt to revivify the Western theosophic and Hermetic traditions,[3] she and her colleague Henry Olcott moved to India in 1879 and forthwith declared themselves Buddhists.[4] They supported the antimissionary movement, encouraging the native peoples to cherish and hold fast to their own Buddhist and Hindu traditions. Shortly afterwards, a pair of mysterious "Mahatmas" (great souls), through Blavatsky's mediation, started to give out quite startling esoteric teachings about the history of the cosmos and the nature of man.[5] These have only recently have been confirmed as coming from Tibetan sources (as Blavatsky always claimed they did).[6]

K. Paul Johnson has argued that Blavatsky's Mahatmas were a front for a dozen or more Hindu, Sikh, Buddhist, and Sufi notables who were engaged in politico-religious machinations.[7] Their political agenda was mainly aimed against the British Empire, which in the late nineteenth century stood for the ultimate in Western arrogance, interference, and exploitation of native peoples. To those aware of the deeper dimensions of their own religious traditions, the injury of colonization was only compounded by the insult of missionaries purporting to save their souls.

Whatever one's opinion about Madame Blavatsky and the Theosophical Society, one fact is beyond dispute: that they alerted the Western public to the riches of Eastern philosophy and religion. Other Orientalists were more scholarly, other Orientals more orthodox than the Mahatmas, but their success came largely because the Theosophists had already paved the way and stimulated a spiritual appetite that the churches could not satisfy. The first such envoy was Vivekananda (1863–1902), a disciple of the great sage Ramakrishna.[8] Vivekananda was a dominating figure at the first World Parliament of Religions (Chicago, 1893), and the first Indian holy man—though by no means the last— to attract a following of wealthy Americans. After his early death, he was followed by others from the Ramakrishna Order, the first Hindu outpost in the New World. Romain Rolland, the Nobel laureate novelist, was much taken with Ramakrishna and Vivekananda, and wrote biographies that emphasized their *bhaktic* nature.[9]

In Hinduism, the *bhakti marga* is one of the three main paths to unity with the Divine. It is the one that leads through love and devotion, hence is the closest to the spirit of Christianity. A very popular vehicle for it for the West was the *Autobiography of a Yogi* by Paramhansa Yogananda.

The *karma marga* with its cognate practice of *karma yoga* is the path of impersonal action. This is the way taught in the Bhagavad-Gita, where Krishna urges Arjuna to do his duty on the battlefield, but without attachment to the fruits of his actions, or hatred of his opponents. Mahatma Gandhi is the most famous modern example of a *karma yogin*. The third way is the *jnana marga*, the way of knowledge or gnosis (*jnana*, knowledge, and gnosis both come from the same Indo-European root). This path has the least popular appeal and visibility, but many people interested in

Eastern philosophy will have heard of Sri Ramana Maharshi (1878–1950).[10] He was the sage of Arunachala whose teaching hinged on the deceptively simple exercise of self-inquiry, pursuing the question "Who/What am I?" to its limit.[11] The yogas that have had the greatest influence in the West are the secondary forms that can be used as adjuncts to any of the paths: *hatha yoga*, which works with body postures and breathing, and *mantra yoga*, which is the basis of "Transcendental Meditation."

The imaginal power behind these techniques and philosophies comes from a notion that was really quite novel to the West: that there are living men and women who have attained the ultimate goal of mankind while still living in the body. Whereas the Christian saint remains distinct from God, in an attitude of love and aspiration, the Hindu sage, we are told, is perpetually conscious of his identity with God (which is the final answer to the question "What am I?"). This is an awe-inspiring idea, and its claimants can only be judged by their fruits. Some of them are in mental institutions. But no one, to my knowledge, has ever questioned the sanity or genuineness of Ramana Maharshi.[12]

The other exemplary aspect of Hinduism is the ease with which it combines philosophical monism with practical polytheism. Hindus worship gods and goddesses of their choice, while freely admitting (if they are philosophical) that these are just aspects of, or emanations from the One. The exclusivity of the Abrahamic religions and the concern about which god(s) one's neighbor is worshipping seem parochial to them.

It is said by traditionalists that a Westerner cannot convert to Hinduism: that the only Hindus are those with the birthright of a particular caste and a way of life conducive to realization. But these principles are breaking down now, as witness the case of Alain Daniélou (1907–1994), born a Frenchman and the brother of a cardinal of the Church, but fully accepted in India as an initiate into the cult of Shiva. Daniélou was a lifelong campaigner for polytheism as the only sensible and genuinely tolerant religion for Westerners and Easterners alike.[13]

The situation is different when we turn to Buddhism, whose various schools show how freely it adapts to different ethnicities. The European and American public got their first positive image of it from Sir Edwin Arnold's epic poem *The Light of Asia* (1879), which was immensely popular in several languages. More detailed appreciation followed, beginning with the Theravada Buddhism of Sri Lanka and Southeast Asia. The first Buddhist missionary to the West was a monk of this school: he was Allan Bennett (1872–1923), sometime magical companion of Aleister Crowley (1875–1947), who trained in Ceylon and came to London in his yellow robes in 1908.[14] But the Theravada school has never had much success in the West. Holding closely to the Buddha's original teachings to his order of monks, it is ascetic in its principles and methods. It allows no immortal soul to man, and, while admitting that there are gods, wants nothing to do with them.

The second school, and the first type of Buddhism to gain wide public recognition, was also an ascetic one: the Zen Buddhism of Japan. Zen's image in the West benefited from the Japanese aesthetic sense that accompanies and derives from it: scroll painting, raku pottery, Noh drama, flower arrangement, the tea ceremony, and the martial trappings of the bowman and the samurai swordsman. Bringing Zen and Japanese culture to the West was virtu-ally the work of one man, the translator and Zen adept D. T. Suzuki (1870–1966). His scholarly and inspiring writings circulated quietly from the 1900s onwards,[15] until after World War II they were discovered and taken up by the artistic avant-garde and the Beatniks (John Cage, Jack Kerouac, Allen Ginsberg, etc.). Thanks to them, and to the writings of the ex–Episcopalian priest Alan Watts, a diluted form of Zen philosophy was fundamental to the counterculture of the 1960s.

Last to arrive was Tibetan Buddhism, whose several rival schools bore the influence of Central Asian shamanism and of Hindu Tantra.[16] As with Zen, there had been a steady influx of scholarly writing and translations before the pro-pitious hour struck for a wider public to take notice. This happened in 1959, when the Fourteenth Dalai Lama fled from the Chinese invasion of Tibet, accompanied or fol-lowed by many of the elite of that theocratic nation. It took another ten years for Tibetan Buddhist centers to form, beginning with Chögyam Trungpa's Naropa Institute in Boulder, Colorado. Since then, interest in and practice of Tibetan Buddhism has rivaled that of Zen in Europe and America, while Theravada has been left standing. Unlike the Japanese way, which wages a solitary battle with the mind, the Tibetan practices are colorful and dramatic, with exotic props like drums made from human skulls and *thangkas* (painted scrolls) of kindly and wrathful deities, often in sexual intercourse. The devotees chant and shout, visualizing the hosts of heaven and hell, all the while feeling empathy with that brave people and the terrible beauty of their land. And there is more: whereas in Hinduism it is rare to meet with a realized sage, and whereas the Zen master is no more than a man or woman, the Tibetan system of *tulkus* (divine incarnations) allows for many teachers of divine status, Western-born as well as Tibetan.

I have concentrated on Hinduism and Buddhism here because they have had a much stronger impact on the Western imagination than Islam and the other Oriental traditions. That is to say, they have impacted as living and life-changing ideas, not merely as objects of curiosity or sentiment (positive or negative, as the case may be). Also they give evidence of a class of people who had become virtually extinct among us: people who do not just radiate sanctity, as many Christians still do, but supreme *knowledge* of the spiritual path, and total, compassionate understanding of the disciple's predicament.

It does seem that the West has done far better out of its colonization of the East than it deserves. It has exported its materialistic values, its hedonistic lifestyle, its hypocritical humanism, and its weaponry, and in return has been offered all the wisdom of the ages! My generation, which came to spiritual awareness in the 1960s and 1970s, has been indelibly marked by this import. Some of us who listened to the wise men from the East, or to the ancient wisdom of the West that resurfaced at the same time, heard things we had been waiting for all our lives. This was not another religion we were being offered, but a philosophy and a method. We were not told to "believe, that ye might know," but to use our own resources to find out the truth for ourselves—and the truth about ourselves.

No one can do this for us; and the "truth" that you find may be different from what I find. We are different facets of universal being, and participate in different aspects of it, the exact mixture constituting our unique and personal equation.[17] In Hinduism, as in Egypt and Greece, these aspects are personified as gods and goddesses, to aid the imagination. Buddhism prefers the negative way, regarding all the facets as illusory; but still they are "real illusions," and the Mahayana, like Tantra, presses them into service as the method for their own dissolution.

In contrast, the Abrahamic religions believe in a single God, creator of heaven and earth, who entered into a covenant with the Children of Israel. The Christians add that he incarnated once and for all in Jesus of Nazareth; the Muslims, that he sent a series of prophets that culminated in the revelation of the Qur'an. If one gives one's heart to any of these historical propositions, one is rewarded by being absorbed into one of the "superfacets" of universal being, in which one will find much comfort and company, in this life and perhaps even after it. Experience will reinforce it, in a mutual exchange of energy between the individual and the group mind. But it demands belief, which is the giving of assent to a proposition one doesn't know to be true. Some people are willing to die, others to kill for these beliefs. Even among esotericists, there comes a point at which consensus breaks down, as each falls back on emotional loyalty to his or her own faith. The view from the distant East, and from our own antiquity, enables one to put all this into perspective, and to see the world of monotheistic faith from the outside. If nothing else, it is a salutary exercise in self-knowledge.

Where does this leave Christianity, once the backbone of Western civilization? First, these reflections are addressed not to the masses of believers or unbelievers, but to the small community of those interested in esoteric matters and willing to question the very ground on which they stand. The answer will depend on the degree to which one sees the Christian religion as linked to the perennial wisdom. If one believes that the perennial wisdom manifests in a series of historical revelations, some of them giving birth to the "great religions," then the latter must be respected and the churches, for all their faults, supported as giving access to the Divine. If on the other hand one holds that a truly perennial wisdom must extend beyond any historical accidents (including the so-called Incarnation), this reduces the churches to the field of social and psychological hygiene. There they may still have value, but are no more relevant to today's philosopher than they were to the Taoists of ancient China.

CHAPTER

16

The End of the Thread?

eturning now to the Western mystery traditions which have been the main subject of this
book, we may well wonder about their pres-
ent condition and prospects. The last link mentioned was
the Theosophical Society, which combined a nineteenth-
century faith in progress with an esoteric scheme of cyclical
history that encouraged cautious optimism. It taught that
humanity had already passed the nadir of spiritual obscurity, turned the corner, and was on the upward path that
would soon see the birth of a new and more enlightened
race.[1] Blavatsky was sure that if the Society's influence were
allowed to flourish, "earth will be a heaven in the twenty-
first century in comparison with what it is now!"[2]

Since those words were written, the Golden Thread has
frayed into a myriad filaments. The Theosophical Society
itself split into several branches, mainly differentiated by

their attitude to Blavatsky's successors, William Q. Judge, Annie Besant, and Charles W. Leadbeater. The Society's erstwhile rival, an organization known as Hermetic Brotherhood of Luxor, faded away, but not before seeding several other movements that offered training in practical occultism, not just theoretical. These include the Ancient and Mystical Order of the Rose Cross (AMORC) and several other orders claiming a Rosicrucian pedigree,[3] the Ordo Templi Orientis (OTO), and the movements influenced by Aleister Crowley. The Hermetic Order of the Golden Dawn also closed its temples, but other magical orders sprouted from it and remain in operation. The seeker who is sufficiently motivated can find them. The same applies to the esoteric groups that can only be entered through Freemasonry. Those who want to learn practical alchemy can seek out the Philosophers of Nature or their successors; those undeterred by a hard and exclusive path can join the Gurdjieff Work. People with a Christian orientation may gravitate to Martinism, or to Rudolf Steiner's Anthroposophy. One no longer has to be Jewish to study the Kabbalah, or Muslim to call oneself a Sufi. Pagans, too, are reviving esoteric teachings and initiatic practices from pre-Christian Europe, especially the Celtic and Northern European strains.

While all these movements can be traced to their roots (and many of them to Theosophy), the twentieth century did see one novel addition to the esoteric tradition, in the form of depth psychology. Carl Jung was mentioned in chapter 13 for his interpretation of alchemy. His neglect of its operative side does not invalidate the insights it gave him into the workings of the psyche, and there are few studies more valuable for the esoteric seeker. Jung showed how we can "know ourselves" to an extent denied to previous generations. To recognize the projections of one's Shadow, to get to know one's Anima, and to spot the telltale signs of inflation in oneself and others (especially spiritual teachers!): that is practical wisdom. The post-Jungian movements, especially those under the general umbrella of Transpersonal Psychology, go further than Jung, as a self-declared scientist, would allow himself in his public work.[4] From them we can discover the subpersonalities contesting within us, and learn to seek the transcendent Self not outside but as the core of our being: advantages of which many a historical adept was unaware. And to study the different personality types, especially with the aid of psychological astrology, goes far towards explaining why people have such different opinions and experiences of reality. However, this emphasis on psychology only reinforces the individualistic nature of the esoteric path in the modern West. There is no central institution, no single curriculum, no diploma of authenticity.

Nowhere is this variety more evident than in the New Age movement: something so fuzzy that one can neither circumscribe nor pinpoint it, while everyone recognizes its symptoms. Scholars now agree that the New Age descends directly from the Hermetic and theosophical currents, of which it is a popularization and exoteric complement.[5] A backward glance at history confirms the diagnosis. Like the Hermetic and Pansophic movements, which hoped to restore peace to Christendom and sanity to warring mankind, the New Age is ecumenical, undogmatic, and pacifistic. Like the alchemists, who believed that all matter is on its way to becoming gold, New Agers are dedicated to personal transformation and the realization of the latent potential in everyone. The occult sciences flourish, admittedly in their shallower modes, in divination systems (Tarot, runes, *I Ching*), astrology, the science of plants (herbal medicine) and stones (crystals). Just as Paracelsus tramped through Europe chatting with woodsmen and wise women, the New Agers seek out and value the wisdom of indigenous peoples. Like any exoteric religion, the New Age has its less praiseworthy aspects. But at its worst it is silly, rather than vicious, and an extraterrestrial observer would find it the most humanistic and earth-friendly of all our current faiths.

The New Age has no scripture, no dogma or ritual, but at its heart is the phenomenon of channeling, whose long history and connection with theurgy was mentioned in chapter 1. Many of the teachings that come through channelers are esoteric in nature, and the phenomenon itself is not so different from that of Blavatsky, Leadbeater, Bailey, or Helena Roerich writing at the Mahatmas' behest; Crowley taking the *Book of the Law* from dictation; W. B. Yeats basing his mythologies on his wife's mediumship; or the anonymous authors of *Oahspe* and *The Urantia Book*. Whether these products derive from the channeler's subconscious mind, or from possession by a separate entity, and what that entity may be, are questions that science might have been able to answer, if it had not turned its back on such matters.[6] As it is, in evaluating channeled teachings one must rely on one's own reason, learning, and intuition, which is a prudent way to approach any scriptures that purport to come from a higher source.

After this outpouring of the esoteric wisdom of all ages and climes, coupled with the personal freedom that many peoples have come to enjoy, some might be inclined to share in the Theosophists' optimism. There is, however, a contrary way of looking at history, and that is the pessimistic view of the Traditionalists. The writings of René Guénon, Ananda K. Coomaraswamy, Julius Evola, Frithjof Schuon, Titus Burckhardt, Philip Sherrard, Martin Lings, and Seyyed Hossein Nasr deplore the modern age as the Kali Yuga, the dark or Iron Age that concludes a superhistorical cycle.[7]

The Traditionalists' "creation myth" was of a Primordial Tradition revealed to prehistoric mankind and descending through the ages in a series of particular revelations. The reader will recognize it as the *prisca theologia,* now expanded to embrace Eastern and native traditions. But while the promoters of the earlier version lived in the heady climate of the Italian Renaissance, the Traditionalists were born to the heyday of modernity. They went on the offensive, unmasking its deceitful myth of progress which blinded people to the dangers of unfettered technology, the impotence of modern philosophy, and the cult of ugliness in the arts. They raged against the tyranny of the economy, which dominates every facet of life under what Guénon called "the reign of quantity."[8] But then, far from recognizing the potential counterbalance of the movements described above, the Traditionalists damned Theosophy and all its derivatives as a "pseudo-religion." They looked on spiritualism with disgust and rejected Jungian psychology on the grounds that it opens the infernal realm of the subconscious and puts the Self in the place of God. Those who lived long enough to see the New Age despised it as a low-grade spiritual supermarket. All they could offer instead was a return to Tradition through adherence to one of the "great religions"—if one could find one still unsullied. Only Evola accepted that in the Kali Yuga there is no tradition left, and that the rare person who aspires to a spiritual path must make his own heroic and lonely way.[9]

The question remains of whether New Age optimism or Traditionalist pessimism is the order of the day. One thing seems sadly evident: that after a century and a half, the exoteric world is still stuck in the dichotomy that Theosophy sought to resolve: the opposition of materialistic science to dogmatic religion. It is almost incredible that towards the end of the twentieth century, biblical fundamentalism made such a comeback in America. No less astounding is its alliance with the small body of Jewish fundamentalists in Israel to further their respective apocalyptic dreams. And then there is Islamic fundamentalism. These frightening movements reduce their parent religions to the lowest and most literal level, which the European intelligentsia—Jews, Christians, and unbelievers alike—discarded two or three centuries ago.[10]

On the other side of the chasm is scientific materialism, which is no less dogmatic in denying the existence of any psychical or spiritual reality. This too has its hysterical defenders, as passionate about their belief as any Bible-thumper, and seething with derision for any who question it as the proper path for mankind.[11] Because the Western democracies are founded on the practice of tolerance, these two parties enjoy an uncomfortable truce in government, the educational world, social life, and even within a single individual.

The twentieth century has come and gone, but neither side has made the slightest progress. Each is mired in a rigorous and dogmatic frame of mind, and as any student of Jungian psychology knows, this causes it to repress the doubts that would naturally and harmlessly occur to a less rigid person, and to project them as a Shadow onto others. For example, in the current debate over whether the universe is the result of "intelligent design," the secularists are terrified that if they give an inch, the religionists will crow with triumph. The religionists are afraid that if they concede a point to Darwinism, their God will become redundant. The tragedy, here as in many other dualistic impasses, is that no one in the public arena can proclaim the third way that transcends them. Such a solution should be possible especially in the United States, whose founding philosophy derived from Freemasonry, and, beyond that, from its Hermetic and Pythagorean parentage.[12] That should have made their people conversant with the idea of the Great Architect of the Universe, not to be confused with that meddling "Old Nobodaddy."[13]

The transcendent philosophy that rises above so many useless arguments has always been there, and never so available as it is today. Knowledge has been put into our hands that was once the closely guarded property of initiates, together with the freedom to discuss and follow it without fear of being executed for heresy. Is this not cause for rejoicing? The price we pay for this historically unique situation is living in the modern world, in which the lunatics quite obviously are running the asylum. So be it. The philosopher knows that the gods are playing their games, the cosmic machinery turns, and history rattles on. But he also knows the timeless, the secret place from which all this can be surveyed with mild amusement, as a flutter on the surface of the ocean.

Notes

CHAPTER 1: The Prisca Theologia

1. For some extraordinary insights into Gemistos, see Christopher Bamford, "The Time-Body of Western Culture," *Lapis* 2 (1995), 41–45.

2. Humanists: students of the *litterae humaniores*, i.e., the (chiefly classical) literature that was not theological or vocational.

3. Ficino, in the preface to his Latin translation of the *Corpus Hermeticum*, gives the following genealogy of the "ancient theologians": Hermes Trismegistus, Orpheus, Aglaophemus, Pythagoras, Philolaus, Plato. In his *Theologia Platonica*, Zoroaster is added at the beginning of the list. See Frances A. Yates, *Giordano Bruno and the Hermetic Tradition* (London: Routledge & Kegan Paul, 1964), 14–15nn. See also the less famous but no less valuable (and readable) work of D. P. Walker, *The Ancient Theology: Studies in Christian Platonism from the Fifteenth to the Eighteenth Century* (London: Duckworth, 1972), 1–21.

4. There is no scholarly consensus about which millennium Zoroaster lived in, or even how many Zoroasters there were.

5. See Stephen Ronan, "Chaldean Hekate," in Ronan, ed., *The Goddess Hekate: Studies in Ancient Pagan and Christian Religion and Philosophy* (Hastings, UK: Chthonios Books, 1992), 1:79–162; The Editors of The Shrine of Wisdom, *The Chaldean Oracles Translated and Systematized with Commentary* (Brook, Surrey, UK: The Shrine of Wisdom, 1979); W. Wynn Westcott, *The Chaldean Oracles of Zoroaster* (Wellingborough, Northamptonshire, UK: Aquarian, 1983), with introduction

by Kathleen Raine; *The Chaldaean Oracles Attributed to Zoroaster as Set Down by Julianus the Theurgist* (Gillette, NJ: Heptangle, 1978), containing Westcott's translation (mainly based on Thomas Taylor's) and Thomas Stanley's translations of commentaries by Plethon and Psellus.

6. Proclus, in his commentary on the *Timaeus*, 3.63.24, states that "it is unlawful to disbelieve" Julianus the Theurgist. (Quoted from the title page of the Heptangle edition.)

7. *Oracle* 178; Aquarian edition, 60; Heptangle edition, 54.

8. Thomas Stanley, *History of Chaldaick Philosophy* (London, 1662), quoted in *Chaldaean Oracles of Julianus*, 76–77; commentary on Oracle 147.

9. The ascension of Enoch: Gen. 5:24; of Elijah: 2 Kings 2:11; of Jesus: Mark 16:19.

10. See the hair-raising account of a contemporary case in Namkhai Norbu, *The Crystal and the Way of Light: Sutra, Tantra, and Dzogchen* (New York: Routledge & Kegan Paul, 1986), 124–29.

11. See Henry Corbin, *Spiritual Body and Celestial Earth from Mazdean Iran to Shi'ite Iran,* trans. Nancy Pearson (Princeton: Princeton/Bollingen, 1977).

12. Shi'ite Islam, prevalent in Iran and Iraq, reveres a series of Imams (spiritual authorities) descended from the Prophet Mohammed. In this respect it differs from Sunni Islam, which prevails in the rest of the Muslim world. On Suhrawardi's debt to pagan philosophy, see Peter Kingsley, "Paths of the Ancient Sages: A Pythagorean History," *Lapis* 10 (1999), 63–68.

13. Corbin, *Spiritual Body and Celestial Earth*, 87.

14. On this, Seyyed Hossein Nasr, a Muslim philosopher and MIT graduate, comments: "For our purpose it is important only to note that since there is, one might say, 'open traffic' between heaven and earth, all questions like miracles, magic, and the

like, which in either Aristotelian or modern rationalistic schools are considered as either too absurd to discuss or too difficult to fit into 'the system,' can be easily placed within the possibilities inherent in the cosmos": Nasr, *An Introduction to Islamic Cosmological Doctrines*, rev. ed. (Boulder, CO: Shambhala, 1978), 91.

15. *The Chaldean Oracles of Zoroaster*, 63.

CHAPTER 2: *The Hermetic Tradition*

1. See Antoine Faivre, *The Eternal Hermes, from Greek God to Alchemical Magus*, trans. J. Godwin (Grand Rapids, MI: Phanes Press, 1995); and Garth Fowden, *The Egyptian Hermes: A Historical Approach to the Late Pagan Mind* (Cambridge: Cambridge University Press, 1986).

2. The standard English translation is Brian Copenhaver, *Hermetica: The Greek Corpus Hermeticum and the Latin Asclepius in a New English Translation* (Cambridge: Cambridge University Press, 1992). Previous versions are by John Everard, *The Divine Pymander of Hermes Mercurius Trismegistus* (London, 1650 and reprints); G. R. S. Mead, *Thrice-Greatest Hermes: Studies in Hellenistic Theosophy and Gnosis*, 3 vols. (London: Theosophical Publishing Society, 1906 and reprints); Walter Scott, *Hermetica: The Ancient Greek and Latin Writings Which Contain Religious or Philosophic Teachings Ascribed to Hermes Trismegistus*, 4 vols. (Oxford: Clarendon Press, 1926 and reprints).

3. See D. P. Walker, *Spiritual and Demonic Magic from Ficino to Campanella* (London: Warburg Institute, 1958), 40–44; Yates, *Giordano Bruno and the Hermetic Tradition*, 66–68.

4. "Poimandres" is sometimes translated as "shepherd of men," but recent scholarship suggests that it is derived not from the Greek *poimen*, "shepherd," but from the Egyptian *pe-men-re*,

meaning "enlightened mind." See Copenhaver, 95.

5. See Normandi Ellis, *Awakening Osiris: The Egyptian Book of the Dead* (Grand Rapids, MI: Phanes Press, 1988), 87–94.

6. See Nick Kollerstrom, "The Star Temples of Harran," in *History and Astrology: Clio and Urania Confer*, ed. A. Kitson (London: Unwin Hyman, 1989), 47–60.

7. See *The Book of Creation*, trans. I. Friedman (New York: Samuel Weiser, 1977).

8. John Michell, *The Temple at Jerusalem: A Revelation* (Glastonbury: Gothic Image, 2000), 60.

9. See *Introduzione alla magia quale scienza dell'Io*, 3 vols. (Genoa: Fratelli Melitta, 1987). A translation of the first volume into English has been published as Julius Evola and the Ur Group, *Introduction to Magic: Rituals and Practical Techniques for the Magus*, trans. G. Stucco, ed. M. Moynihan (Rochester, VT: Inner Traditions International, 2000); J. Godwin, "The Survival of the Personality According to Modern Esoteric Teachings," in *Ésotérisme, Gnoses & Imaginaire Symbolique, Mélanges offerts à Antoine Faivre*, ed. R. Caron, J. Godwin, W. J. Hanegraaff, J. L. Viellard-Baron (Louvain, Belgium: Peeters, 2001), 403–14.

10. See Ea [Julius Evola], "The Doctrine of the 'Immortal Body'," in *Introduction to Magic*, 196–202.

11. H. P. Blavatsky, "Death and Immortality," *Collected Writings* (Wheaton, IL: Theosophical Publishing House, 1969), 4:250–56.

CHAPTER 3: *The Orphic Mysteries*

1. See John Michell, *The New View over Atlantis* (London: Thames & Hudson, 1987).

2. Jean Richer, *Sacred Geometry of the Ancient Greeks: Astrological Symbolism in Art, Architecture, and Landscape*, trans. Christine Rhone (Albany: State University of New York Press, 1994).

3. Paul Broadhurst and Hamish Miller, *The Dance of the Dragon: An Odyssey into Earth Energies and Ancient Religion* (Launceston, UK: Pendragon Press, 2000).

4. John Michell and Christine Rhone, *Twelve-Tribe Nations and the Science of Enchanting the Landscape* (London: Thames & Hudson, 1991).

5. See *The Ancient Mysteries: A Sourcebook: Sacred Texts of the Mystery Religions of the Ancient Mediterranean World*, ed. M. W. Meyer (San Francisco: Harper & Row, 1987); Walter Burkert, *Ancient Mystery Cults* (Cambridge, MA: Harvard University Press, 1987).

6. Notably in Ovid, *Metamorphoses,* book 11.

7. Scholarly, bilingual edition by Apostolos N. Athanassakis, *The Orphic Hymns: Text, Translation and Notes* (Missoula, MT: Scholars Press, 1977). For a poetic rendering, see *The Hymns of Orpheus: Mutations by R.C. Hogart* (Grand Rapids, MI: Phanes Press, 1993).

8. *Odyssey,* 11:601–4.

9. For the texts, see Kathleen Freeman, *Ancilla to the Pre-Socratic Philosophers* (Cambridge, MA: Harvard University Press, 1957), 5–7. A recent study: Hans Dieter Betz, "'Der Erde Kind bin ich und des gestirnten Himmels': Zur Lehre vom Menschen in den orphischen Goldplättchen," in *Ansichten griechischer Rituale für Walter Burkert* (Stuttgart: B. G. Teubner, 1998), 399–419.

10. Ovid, *Metamorphoses,* 11:1–85.

11. For an overview, see J. Godwin, *Mystery Religions in the Ancient World* (London: Thames & Hudson, 1981).

12. Friedrich Loofs, "Descent to Hades (Christ's)," in *Encyclopaedia of Religion and Ethics,* ed. J. Hastings, (Edinburgh: T. & T. Clark, 1911), 4:654–63.

13. See William Stirling, *The Canon: An Exposition of the Pagan Mystery Perpetuated in the Cabala as the Rule of All the Arts* (first ed., 1897, reprinted London: Garnstone Press, 1974); John Michell, *The Dimensions of Paradise: The Proportions and Symbolic Numbers of Ancient Cosmology,* (London: Thames & Hudson, 1988); David Fideler, *Jesus Christ, Sun of God* (Wheaton, IL: Quest, 1993).

14. The nine Muses first appear in Hesiod, *Theogony,* 77–79. Their attributes and subjects appear in later sources and vary, but are usually: Calliope, epic song; Clio, history; Euterpe, lyric song; Thalia, comedy; Melpomene, tragedy; Terpsichore, dance; Erato, erotic poetry (or geometry); Polyhymnia, sacred song; Urania, astronomy.

15. See Michell and Rhone.

16. See P. Devereux, *Stone Age Soundtracks: The Acoustic Archaeology of Ancient Sites* (London: Vega, 2001).

17. See the *Yueh Chi* or *Record of Music,* part of the *Li Chi: Book of Rites* (New Hyde Park, NY: University Books, 1967), 2:92–131.

18. See Anthony Aveni, "Astronomy in Ancient Mesoamerica," in *In Search of Ancient Astronomies,* ed. E. C. Krupp (New York: Doubleday, 1978), 165–202.

19. In Plato, *Republic* 5, 473d.

20. Suzi Gablik, "The Unmaking of a Modernist," *Lapis* 8 (1999), 25–27; here 26.

21. See Stephan A. Hoeller, *Freedom: Alchemy for a Voluntary Society* (Wheaton, IL: Quest, 1992), 168–76.

CHAPTER 4: *Pythagoras and His School*

1. These tales are reported by his biographers Iamblichus and Porphyry, whose lives of Pythagoras are collected, with much else, in *The Pythagorean Sourcebook and Library,* compiled and translated by K. S. Guthrie, ed. D. Fideler (Grand Rapids, MI: Phanes Press, 1987). Much insight can be gained from the modern retellings of Pythagoras's life: Peter Gorman, *Pythagoras: A Life* (London: Routledge & Kegan Paul, 1979); John Strohmeier and Peter Westbrook, *Divine Harmony: The Life and Teachings of Pythagoras* (Berkeley: Berkeley Hills Books, 1999).

2. That in a right triangle, the square of the hypotenuse is equal to the sum of the squares on the other two sides.

3. If one takes musical strings of these relative lengths, assuming that their thickness and tension are equal, they will sound the intervals of an octave (12:6), a fifth (12:8 and 9:6), and a fourth (12:9 and 8:6), which are the perfect consonances of ancient and medieval music theory. All Greek and Western European scales are based on this matrix of consonances; hence these four numbers are the foundation of our music.

4. There is ample evidence for this in the writings of Ernest G. McClain, especially *The Myth of Invariance: The Origins of the Gods, Mathematics and Music From the Rg Veda to Plato* (New York: Nicolas Hays, 1976). In his later work, McClain shows that the mathematics of musical tuning systems was also understood by the compilers of the Hebrew scriptures in the sixth century BC, thus supporting the theory that Pythagoras learned it from the Babylonians at around the same time. See E. G. McClain, "A Priestly View of Bible Arithmetic: Deity's Regulative Aesthetic Activity Within Davidic Musicology," in *Hermeneutic Philosophy of Science, Van Gogh's Eyes, and God: Essays in Honor of Patrick A. Heelan, S. J.,* ed. Babette E. Barach (Dordrecht, Netherlands: Kluwer, 2001), 429–43.

5. This was proved by the measurements and calculations of

Alexander Thom. See his *Megalithic Sites in Britain* (Oxford: Clarendon Press, 1967).

6. See illustrations and analyses in Keith Critchlow, *Time Stands Still: New Light on Megalithic Science* (London: Gordon Fraser, 1979), 112–130; Michael Poynder, *Pi in the Sky: A Revelation of the Ancient Wisdom Tradition* (London: Rider, 1992), 133–65.

7. The most usual explanation for this setback is the eruption of the volcanic island of Thera (or Santorini) in about 1450 B.C. See J. V. Luce, *Lost Atlantis: New Light on an Old Legend* (London: Thames & Hudson, 1969).

8. There is a technical distinction between the well-known term "reincarnation" and the one used by the Pythagoreans: "metempsychosis." The latter concerns the changing states of the *psyche*, commonly translated as "soul" but better envisaged as "soul-stuff," a divisible substance released at death from its bond with the body. This substance can then animate another body, or bodies, human or animal. Reincarnation, on the other hand, is usually understood to mean the return of an individual soul to the human state. The classic treatment of this question in modern times is in chapter 6 of René Guénon, *L'erreur spirite,* 2nd ed. (Paris: Éditions Traditionnelles, 1952), 206–211. For an impartial clarification of the issues, see J. Godwin, "The Case against Reincarnation," in *Gnosis* 42 (1997), 27–32.

9. This is the conclusion suggested by the studies collected in J. Godwin, "The Survival of the Personality, According to Modern Esoteric Teachings." (See chapter 2, note 8.)

10. Many readers will recognize the same imagery, illustrating the same principles, in Buddhism.

11. See C. Kerényi, "The Secret of Eleusis," in his *Eleusis: Archetypal Image of Mother and Daughter,* trans. R. Manheim (New York: Bollingen, 1967) 67–102; Walter Burkert, "The Extraordinary Experience," in his *Ancient Mystery Cults,*

89–114. These two scholars go far in trying to penetrate the mysteries of Eleusis.

12. *Harper's Dictionary of Classical Literature and Antiquities* (New York: American Book Co., 1896), s.v. "Eleusinia."

13. The medieval Seven Liberal Arts included the Pythagorean curriculum in the Quadrivium: the four "arts" of Arithmetic, Geometry, Music, and Astronomy. These succeeded the Trivium of verbal arts: Grammar, Rhetoric, and Logic.

14. See J. Godwin, *Music and the Occult: French Musical Philosophies, 1750–1950* (Rochester, NY: University of Rochester Press, 1994), for a survey of modern Pythagorean approaches to music; also *Harmony of the Spheres: A Sourcebook of the Pythagorean Tradition in Music,* ed. J. Godwin (Rochester, VT: Inner Traditions, 1993), which gathers the older evidence.

CHAPTER 5: *Plato's Cave*

1. Credit for filling them is largely due to the work of Peter Kingsley, beginning with his study of Parmenides (c. 515–after 450 B.C.), *In the Dark Places of Wisdom* (Inverness, CA: Golden Sufi Center, 1999).

2. See Plato, *Republic* 6, 505–9.

3. This was developed in especial detail by Proclus in his various commentaries on Plato's dialogues, and, following these, by Thomas Taylor in his "Apology for the Fables of Homer," in his edition of Plato, *Works* (London, 1804), 1:133–199, especially 182–190; reprinted in Kathleen Raine and George Mills Harper, eds., *Thomas Taylor the Platonist: Selected Writings* (Princeton: Princeton University Press, 1969), 449–520.

4. See e.g. Plotinus, *Enneads* 3.5; 5.8.

5. This is the mythical "Great Chain of Being," celebrated by Arthur O. Lovejoy, *The Great Chain of Being: A Study of the History of an Idea* (Cambridge, MA: Harvard University Press, 1964).

6. See *Republic* 6, 510–11, for the simile of the "divided line" explaining the different modes of knowledge and their respective objects; *Enneads* 4.4.24–26 for some developments of the idea.

7. The Myth of the Cave is in *Republic* 7, 514–17.

8. Six academicians, including Simplicius, were protected by King Khosroes, who ensured through a treaty with the Byzantine Empire that the philosophers would not be molested when they returned to their homeland in 560.

9. As argued by the Emperor Julian in his *Against the Galileans,* and by Porphyry in a lost work of similar title. (They did not, of course, refer to Islam.)

10. Plato, *Apology of Socrates*, 21d.

11. Illustrated to perfection in Plato's *Laches.*

12. E.g. the Myth of the Cave, already mentioned, and the Myth of Er in *Republic* 614–19: the Myth of the Charioteer in *Phaedrus* 246–49; the Myth of the True Earth in *Phaedo,* 107–114. Of course, Plato may have used Socrates as a literary device to convey myths of his own invention.

13. Plato's *Meno* is dedicated to this thesis, demonstrating through the questioning of a slave boy that everyone possesses innate knowledge of the laws of geometry.

14. The definitive statement of this is in Socrates's report of the wise woman Diotima's speech in Plato, *Symposium,* 206–9.

15. Plotinus develops this further in *Enneads* 3.5.

16. The opening salvo was an attack on Plato in Karl Popper, *The

Open Society and Its Enemies (London: Routledge, 1947). Plato's low opinion of democracy is voiced by Socrates in *Republic* 557–62. A political analysis of Socrates's trouble as stemming from his support of the aristocratic party in Athens is I. F. Stone, *The Trial of Socrates* (New York: Doubleday, 1989), esp. 140–56.

CHAPTER 6: *The Power of the Egregore*

1. On ancient Roman religion, beside works cited in chapter 3, see Robert Turcan, *The Gods of Ancient Rome* (New York: Routledge, 2001). I am also indebted to Italian sources, such as Julius Evola, *La Tradizione di Roma* (n.p: Edizioni di Ar, 1977), and many articles in the journal *Politica Romana* (1991–), on which see note 8 below.

2. Thus the old Roman religion formed part of the broader European family of polytheistic religions, later misnamed "paganisms" (=peasant religions). A sympathetic study in a phenomenological spirit is Ken Dowden, *European Paganism: The Realities of Cult from Antiquity to the Middle Ages* (London: Routledge, 2000).

3. My book *Mystery Religions in the Ancient World* sought to remedy this by taking those religions on their own merits and showing their convergence with five universal paths of religious aspiration: those of the warrior, the ascetic, the magician, the devotee, and the philosopher.

4. Like *paganus* in Roman times, "occultist" is not usually a complimentary term. Current academic usage, reluctant to concede any validity to what the word represents, restricts it to those who used the term of themselves: nineteenth-century students and practitioners of the "occult sciences," mostly French, and their successors, including many Theosophists. However, the term remains useful in other contexts, especially to distinguish occultists from esotericists. Esotericism usually presupposes a

corresponding *exo*tericism, i.e., a religion. Occultism does not depend on religious belief, but on the conviction that there are forces, properties of matter, human capabilities, and/or beings who are "occulted" or hidden from the normal senses. As Dowden's book illustrates, much paganism is occultism far more than it is religion. Its aim is to work a system of cause and effect, rather than the "re-linking" (*religio*) of self with divinity. See also a recent study by an expert on new religious movements: PierLuigi Zocatelli, "Note per uno studio scientifico dell'esoterismo," in G. Giordan, ed., *Tra religione e spiritualità: Il rapporto con il sacro nell'epoca del pluralismo* (Milan: Franco Angeli, 2006), 222–34.

5. On the concept of the egregore, which was most current in nineteenth-century French occultism, see the anonymous *Meditations on the Tarot: A Journey into Christian Hermeticism,* trans. R. A. Powell (Warwick, NY: Amity House, 1985), 419.

6. First published 1776–88.

7. A very well-illustrated book on Mithraism and its sanctuaries, written in the spirit of modern Italian Neopaganism, is Carlo Pavia, *Guida dei Mitrei di Roma antica: Dai misteriosi sotterranei della Capitale; Oro, incenso e Mithra* (Rome: Gangemi Editore, 1999).

8. This is not to say that they might not be revived, as might the other supposedly defunct nodes of collective energy mentioned here. For C. G. Jung, the archetypes were real entities, but an understandable avoidance of occultism kept him from speculation about their objective existence. Jung's writings on the dormancy and resurgence of the Wotan archetype bear on this question. He wrote in these essays about the return of Wotan or Odin, the Germanic god of storm and initiation, first in the dreams of Jung's German patients, then in the *völkisch* movements and in National Socialism. See his *Essays on Contemporary Events,* trans. E. Welsh et al. (London: Kegan Paul, 1947).

   A case is made for the partial revival of the pagan gods in

the Renaissance in J. Godwin, *The Pagan Dream of the Renaissance* (Grand Rapids, MI: Phanes Press, 2002). In Italy after World War I there was a concerted effort to restore the ancient Roman religion, led by Arturo Reghini and supported, for a time, by the young Julius Evola, whose *Imperialismo pagano* (1928) is a forceful defense of pagan imperialism against its Christian supplanter. Evidence of more recent activities emerges from the journal *Politica Romana,* which serves as a forum for a number of distinguished scholars and thinkers including the late Marco Baistrocchi (a diplomat by profession), Piero Fenili (a judge), and the expatriate American Dana Lloyd Thomas. Roman religion appears there in a broad context of philosophical polytheism, keeping company with Mahayana Buddhism, Vedanta, and Neoplatonism. The feasts of the Roman calendar are commemorated, the gods and sacred sites of the city are honored, and the Italian Renaissance and the Masonically-inspired Risorgimento are celebrated as manifestations of the original spirit of Italy. An effort in a similar direction was the journal *Antaios,* edited by Mircea Eliade and Ernst Jünger. Avowedly polytheistic, *Antaios* aimed at a Europe of mutually respectful homelands rejoicing in their ancestral myths, their gods and goddesses, and in the earth from which, in the Greek legend, the giant Antaios derived his strength. A third example of a philosophically-based Neopagan enterprise is the Asatru movement, devoted to the revival of the Nordic gods, whose most active and erudite spokesman is Edred Thorsson (Stephen E. Flowers).

9. There is a distinction to be made between gods as egregores of human creation and gods as beings in their own right who have some relationship with humans. In the latter case, there is a further distinction of rank between what the Neoplatonists called the "deific" and the "daimonic" orders. As so often happens, light from the East helps to sort this out. Here is Marco Pallis, authority on Tibet and on comparative religion, on the subject: "The gods here [on the Buddhist Wheel or Round of Existence] referred to are not immortal and self-sufficient deities, but simply beings of an Order higher than ours, pos-

sessed of wider powers than man's such as longevity, unfading beauty, and freedom from pain, except at the last when they are about to cease from being gods and turn into something lower; for then their charms begin to wither and their fragrance turns to stench so foul, that their goddess-wives flee from their presence. . . . 'Many long-lived gods are fools,' said a lama to me. . . . It would have saved some confusion if we could have called these gods 'supermen' or 'angels' or some such name. Technically speaking, they should have their full denomination of 'Gods of the Round' (to worship whom is idolatry), to distinguish them from true Divinities, those who are free of the Round, Buddhas and high degrees on the road to Buddhahood." M. Pallis, *Peaks and Lamas* (New York: Alfred A. Knopf, 1940), 152.

CHAPTER 7: *The Meddling God*

1. For a survey that treats both the history of Gnosticism and the infusion of Gnostic ideas in popular culture, see Richard Smoley, *Forbidden Faith: The Gnostic Legacy from the Gospels to The Da Vinci Code* (San Francisco: Harper San Francisco, 2006).

2. *Republic,* 6, 509–11.

3. The name for the image-making function is *eikasia*. Plato seems to include here both mental images and external ones that have no physical reality, such as shadows and reflections (ibid., 510a).

4. This is *pistis,* which takes the objects of sense (Plato names animals, plants, and manmade things) and forms opinions about them (ibid.).

5. This is *dianoia,* which also works with sense objects (including geometrical figures), but makes investigations and draws rational conclusions from them (ibid., 510d–e).

6. Plato uses the term *noesis*. His text is very obscure at this point (511b), but suggests that this function gives knowledge not of sense objects but of the Forms themselves. English translators do not agree on how to name the four functions. Thomas Taylor calls them "passions of the soul," and names them from the top downwards: 1. Intelligence; 2. the Dianoëtic Part; 3. Faith; 4. Assimilation (*Works,* 1804, 1:356). Paul Shorey's translation of 1930 calls them "affections occurring in the soul" and names them: 1. Intellection or Reason; 2. Understanding; 3. Belief; 4. Picture Thinking or Conjecture: in Plato, *The Collected Dialogues,* ed. E. Hamilton and H. Cairns (Princeton: Princeton/Bollingen, 1961), 747. G. M. A. Grube's version, much used in college teaching, has "processes in the soul" and calls them: 1. Understanding; 2. Reasoning; 3. Opinion; 4. Imagination. This shows how futile it is to conduct any serious study from translated sources.

7. I cite this *locus classicus* of the Jung mythology from Richard Smoley and Jay Kinney, *Hidden Wisdom: A Guide to the Western Inner Traditions*, rev ed. (Wheaton, IL: Quest, 2006), 19. The recent smear campaign against Jung by Freudians and other counter-Gnostics has succeeded in conformist academe, but Jung's greatness will doubtless outlast them all.

8. See Douglas Harding, *On Having No Head: A Contribution to Zen in the West* (London: Buddhist Society, 1961 and reissues).

9. In 1995 the late John Wren-Lewis kindly let me read the manuscript of his book *The 9:15 to Nirvana*. One could not expect such a train to leave on time; publication was last announced for 2005.

10. And some get along very well with almost none. See the remarkable medical report: Robert Wesson, "Is Your Brain Really Necessary?" *Science*, 210 (1980), 1232; cited in William R. Corliss, *Biological Anomalies: Humans II* (Glen Arm, MD: Sourcebook Project, 1993), 265–66.

11. Quoted in Plato, *Gorgias,* 493a.

12. Plato has Socrates say: "Every seeker after wisdom knows that up to the time when philosophy takes it over his soul is a helpless prisoner, chained hand and foot in the body . . ." (*Phaedo*, 83e, trans. H. Tredennick; in Tredennick and H. Tarrant, *The Last Days of Socrates*, New York: Penguin, 1954).

13. The description of the ascent through the spheres is in the *Poimandres, Corpus Hermeticum* 1, 25–26a.

14. See *Poimandres*, 14, and works of Gnostic literature such as *Pistis Sophia* and the *Hymn of the Robe of Glory*. The works of G. R. S. Mead (who translated and edited the works mentioned) are a mine of valuable sources and reflections on these matters, with comparisons drawn from Eastern philosophy. While the latter is of no relevance to "pure" scholarship (hence the banishment of Mead from academic discourse), it is of considerable interest to those who think that these are literally matters of life and death. A vivid description of the soul's obscuration and descent through the spheres is in the third–fourth century Neoplatonist Aristeides Quintilianus. See his *On Music, in Three Books*, ed. and trans. Thomas Mathiesen (New Haven, CT: Yale University Press, 1983), 151–52.

15. "Everyone will see that [the Demiurge] must have looked to the eternal [for his model], for the world is the fairest of creatures and he is the best of causes" (*Timaeus*, 29a).

16. See, for example, "On the Origin of the World" in *The Nag Hammadi Library in English*, ed. J. M. Robinson (San Francisco: Harper & Row, 1977), 163.

17. "Celsus [...] reports that the Gnostics—he considers them Christians—called the God of the Jews the 'accursed God,' since he created the visible world and withheld knowledge from men." Kurt Rudolph, *Gnosis: The Nature and History of an Ancient Religion* (Edinburgh: T. & T. Clark, 1983), 73, with reference to Origen, *Contra Celsum*, 6.28.

18. Philip Pullman, *The Amber Spyglass* (London: Scholastic, 2000; part 3 of the trilogy *His Dark Materials*).

19. *Poimandres*, 24, trans. Scott. Pullman's Gnosticism however only goes halfway, because his ultimate reality is not transcendent but pantheistic. See J. Godwin, "Esotericism without Religion in Philip Pullman's *His Dark Materials,*" forthcoming in *Tyr* 3 (2007).

20. In "The Second Treatise of the Great Seth," Jesus laughs at the Demiurge's pretensions: "And then a voice—of the Cosmocrator—came to the angels: 'I am God and there is no other beside me.' But I laughed joyfully when I examined his empty glory." *Nag Hammadi Library in English,* 331.

21. Thanks to Henry Corbin and his translators, this tradition has been made accessible in modern Europe. See chapter 2, note 8, and, in the present context, Corbin's *The Man of Light in Iranian Sufism,* trans. Nancy Pearson (Boulder, CO: Shambhala, 1978).

22. This summary draws on Fred. J. Powicke's "Bogomils" in *Encyclopaedia of Religion and Ethics,* 2:784–85, and on standard encyclopedic sources.

23. On Gnosticism since the nineteenth-century occult revival see Massimo Introvigne, *Il ritorno dello gnosticismo* (Carnago, Italy: SugarCo Edizioni, 1993), unfortunately not yet translated.

24. Author of *Chariots of the Gods?,* first published 1968, trans. M. Heron (New York: G. P. Putnam's Sons, 1970), and many subsequent books on the same theme. The unsubtlety of this author and his imitators consists partly in their crass materialism, and, even given that constriction, in the poverty of their imaginations, which are unable to go beyond the limits of early human space travel. Thus, for instance, von Däniken's spacemen wore helmets and needed to have their landing strips marked out for them by the Stone Age inhabitants of earth. In this as in many other fields of "rejected knowledge," the treatment by popular writers and by the media has given the kiss of death to any serious investigation.

25. This is written with a sympathetic nod to those who long to

find spiritual guidance, and who either find none, or fall into the hands of self-deluded or cynical "masters." Even genuinely wise and illuminated persons can sometimes be hopeless as psychologists and advisors; see the examples in Anthony Storr, *Feet of Clay: Saints, Sinners, and Madmen: A Study of Gurus* (New York: Free Press, 1996). There is no easy solution, as witness the Buddha's parting words: "Be a light unto yourselves." On spiritual mentorship in original Gnosticism and Hermetism, see Peter Kingsley, "An Introduction to the *Hermetica*: Approaching Ancient Esoteric Tradition," in *From Poimandres to Jacob Böhme: Gnosis, Hermetism and the Christian Tradition,* ed. R. van den Broek and C. van Heertum (Amsterdam: in de Pelikaan, 2000), 17–40.

26. A superabundance of anti-Darwinian evidence is presented in Michael Cremo and Richard L. Thompson, *Forbidden Archaeology: The Hidden History of the Human Race* (San Diego: Bhaktivedanta Institute, 1993).

27. The archaeologist and psychical researcher T. C. Lethbridge made a tentative start in his last book, *The Legend of the Sons of God: A Fantasy?* (London: Routledge & Kegan Paul, 1972). A serious investigation would have to take into account the copious writings on this subject by H. P. Blavatsky, especially *The Secret Doctrine* (London: Theosophical Publishing Co., 1888), vol. 2, "Anthropogenesis." There are several separate hypotheses to be considered: 1. That the mutation which brought *homo sapiens sapiens* into being was deliberately introduced by an entity or entities unknown. (This is a major theme of Zechariah Sitchin's books, beginning with *The Twelfth Planet,* New York: Stein & Day, 1976.) 2. That early man was educated by superior beings from elsewhere, later commemorated as "gods" (a pioneering treatment is Brinsley le Poer Trench, *Men Among Mankind,* London: Neville Spearman, 1962; see also Lethbridge, op. cit., and Robert K. G. Temple, *The Sirius Mystery* (New York: St. Martin's Press, 1976), 3. That the motivation of such beings may not have been in mankind's best interests (see for instance Kenneth Grant,

Outside the Circles of Time, London: Frederick Muller, 1980, and, more amusingly, Pierre Gripari, *Histoire du méchant Dieu,* Paris: L'Age d'Homme, 1979); 4. That they are still engaged with us, perhaps as the "unknown superiors" of occult groups, perhaps as the aliens who perform abductions (see Valdemar Valerian, *The Matrix,* 5 vols. (Yelm, WA: Leading Edge Research Group, 1992–2006). The mythos of Scientology is also relevant here.

CHAPTER 8: *The Negative Theology*

1. In the Middle Ages, three different persons named Dionysius were believed to be a single one: 1. The author of the *Celestial Hierarchies,* who was probably a Christian pupil of Damascius, the last teacher of the Athenian Academy, hence active around 500; 2. The Athenian convert mentioned in Acts 17:34: "Some men joined [Paul], among them Dionysius the Areopagite." 3. St. Dionysius or Denis, the patron saint of France, who probably lived in the early third century. Hence the mystical author is traditionally referred to as "Pseudo-Dionysius the Areopagite."

2. Dionysius the Areopagite, *Mystical Theology and the Celestial Hierarchies* (Brook, Surrey, UK: Shrine of Wisdom, 1965), 10.

3. Ibid., 9.

4. Ibid., 11, translation adapted.

5. Ibid., 10.

6. The orders are, from the top down: Seraphim, Cherubim, Thrones; Dominions, Virtues, Powers; Principalities, Archangels, Angels.

7. I.e., the gods and daimons of Neoplatonism. For insights into the process, and a much-needed defense of the Neoplatonic philosopher and theurgist Iamblichus, see Leonard George,

"The Teachings of Iamblichus: Between Eros and Anteros," *Lapis* 13 (2001), 61–66. George argues that Dionysius "recast the invisible hierarchy personifying the circulation of Eros as nine angelic choirs" (66).

8. The edition cited, 70–73, gives examples from later mystics who echoed Dionysius.

9. See Christopher Bamford's introduction to John Scotus Eriugena, *The Voice of the Eagle: Homily on the Prologue to the Gospel of St. John* (Hudson, NY: Lindisfarne, 1991), 8–9.

10. Ibid., 26.

11. A recent study is Reiner Schürmann, *Wandering Joy: Meister Eckhart's Mystical Philosophy* (Great Barrington, MA: Lindisfarne, 2001).

12. Franz Pfeiffer, *Meister Eckhart*, trans. C. de B. Evans (London: Watkins, 1924), 1:291. Notice the imagery of the golden chain suspended from the highest God (ultimately derived from Homer, *Iliad*, 9.27), and the strong flavor of Neoplatonic cosmic hierarchy and harmony.

13. In Platonism the three are *nous, psyche,* and *soma.* A single echo of this remains in St. Paul, who commends his readers "*pneuma, psyche,* and *soma.*" (1 Thess. 5:23). Why he preferred *pneuma* to *nous* is a question for experts to argue over.

14. For instance, in the copious writings of Marsilio Ficino about the *spiritus* and its cultivation.

15. This was the subject of Jung's last book, *Mysterium Coniunctionis,* trans. R. F. C. Hull (Princeton: Princeton/Bollingen, 1963).

16. Perhaps it would be truer to say that those who laid down the path, for the better control of their flocks, strayed from the original, unestablished, gnostic Christianity.

17. "They say: 'God has begotten a son.' You have uttered a grievous thing, which would cleave the skies asunder, rend the earth,

and split the mountains, for they have attribute a son to Ar-Rahman, when it does not behove the Merciful to have a son." Qur'an 19:88–92 (*Sacred Writings: Islam, The Qur'an*, trans. Ahmed Ali, Princeton: Princeton University Press, 1988, 265).

18. Efforts to fit the universe into rational systems and schemata are doomed to provinciality, none agreeing with any other. At the present stage of human intelligence, we have no more chance of success than an ant with a theory about human society. When the rational mind is bypassed by gnosis, the result is "ineffable" (inexpressible in words), and paradoxically most certain; but that has nothing to do with categories of thought, molded as those are by genetics, language, and the senses.

CHAPTER 9: *Cathedrals of Light*

1. The following summary is based on chapter 4 of Dionysius the Areopagite, *The Divine Names,* trans. Editors of the Shrine of Wisdom (Brook, Surrey, UK: Shrine of Wisdom, 1957), 30–34.

2. The association of Gothic architecture with light mysticism is one of the main themes of Otto von Simson, *The Gothic Cathedral: Origins of Gothic Architecture and the Medieval Concept of Order* (New York: Bollingen, 1962), esp. 52–55. Von Simson's was one of the many works of "inspired scholarship" published in the Bollingen series, which was financed by the Mellon family and named after the village in which Carl Jung's retreat was located. See also the sometimes exasperating but suggestive work of Louis Charpentier, *The Mysteries of Chartres Cathedral,* trans. R. Fraser (London: Research into Lost Knowledge Organization, 1972), esp. 137–43.

3. Von Simson, 119n.

4. See the oft-reproduced illustration from a thirteenth-century French *Bible moralisée* now in Vienna, e.g. in von Simson, pl.

6a. William Blake echoed this theme in his watercolors *The Ancient of Days* and *Isaac Newton.*

5. Thierry of Chartres, cited in von Simson, 27.

6. On gematria, see the references in chapter 3, note 14.

7. See John James, *Chartres: The Masons Who Built a Legend* (London: Routledge & Kegan Paul, 1982), 108.

8. See Charpentier, esp. 86–87; R. A. Schwaller de Lubicz, *The Temple in Man: The Secrets of Ancient Egypt,* trans. R. & D. Lawlor (Brookline, MA: Autumn Press, 1977), 39–41; the Schwaller-influenced Robert Lawlor, *Sacred Geometry, Philosophy and Practice* (London: Thames & Hudson, 1982), 23–37; also the Theosophically based L. Gordon Plummer, *The Mathematics of the Cosmic Mind* (Wheaton, IL: Theosophical Publishing House, 1970), 179–88.

9. There had been rich traditions of polyphony before the Notre-Dame school and its first named composer, Magister Leoninus (or Léonin), e.g. in Winchester, in the Aquitaine region, and in Santiago de Compostela, to say nothing of the oral traditions that are lost to us. See any standard history of music, but especially Richard Taruskin, *The Oxford History of Western Music* (Oxford: Oxford University Press, 2005), 1:147–68.

10. Notably the motet, which, as its name (from French *mot*) indicates, originated from the putting of sacred or secular words to the liturgical pieces of the Notre Dame school. The motet became the primary vehicle for thirteenth-century polyphonic composers, and the laboratory in which they developed new resources of rhythm and harmony.

11. For example, taking any note C as 1, this would give the chord above it of C, G, C, and E. Taking the numbers in the opposite direction, with string ratios of 1, 2, 3, 4, and 5, gives the minor triad: C, C, F, C, A-flat.

12. Composers like César Franck, Louis Vierne, Gabriel Pierné,

NOTES TO PAGE 82

Louis Widor, and Olivier Messiaen, whose brilliant figurations and quick harmonic changes become blurred in a resonant church.

13. This was first brought to general attention in the 1970s by David Hykes and his Harmonic Choir, who used Tibetan or Mongolian vocal techniques to focus the harmonics naturally occurring in song, and recorded Hykes's compositions in the Abbey of Le Thoronet, a smallish but acoustically extraordinary church. One should also mention Karlheinz Stockhausen's six-voice piece *Stimmung*, based on harmonics, and what must have been a most memorable performance in 1969 in the Jeita Cavern, Lebanon. See Stockhausen's *Texte zur Musik 1963–1970* (Cologne: DuMont Schauberg, 1971), 360.

14. Beginning with Henry Adams, *Mont Saint-Michel and Chartres* (Boston: Houghton Mifflin, 1904).

15. It is significant that churches and cathedrals were built on sites already hallowed by pagans, who had chosen sites at which the energies of the earth were particularly strong or beneficial. A convincing and, in its way, scientific test of this principle is Paul Broadhurst and Hamish Miller, *The Dance of the Dragon* (see chapter 3, note 2). The authors traveled in stages from Skellig Saint Michael, off the west coast of Ireland, to the island of Delos and eventually to Armageddon (Megiddo, in northern Israel), following an alignment of sacred sites and plotting its underlying currents. The major sites in France included Mont Saint-Michel, the cathedrals of Le Mans, Bourges, and Nevers, the shrine of Paray-le-Monial, and the abbey of Cluny.

16. The first version of the present book (see preface) was titled *Annals of the Invisible College,* referring to the belief that there is a group of sages or "Unknown Superiors" who oversee civilizations and care for the spiritual welfare of humanity. The Rosicrucian movement makes the most explicit use of this idea, which is easily projected back into the past, and to the cathedral builders as Freemasons *avant la lettre.*

CHAPTER 10: *The Arts of the Imagination*

1. See Marsha Keith Schuchard, *Restoring the Temple of Vision: Cabalistic Freemasonry and Stuart Culture* (Boston: Brill, 2002).

2. See Abraham Abulafia's system, as explained in Aryeh Kaplan, *Meditation and Kabbalah* (York Beach, ME: Samuel Weiser, 1982).

3. See Nasr, 50–51, which gives the letter-number correspondences as used by the tenth-century Ikhwan al-Safa (Brethren of Purity) and other Sufi sects for scriptural interpretation.

4. See Frances A. Yates, *The Art of Memory* (Chicago: University of Chicago Press, 1966), 113–23 *et passim*.

5. Specifically from the account of the building of the Temple of Solomon (1 Kings 5–9), to which Masonic mythology adds an apocryphal tale of the slaying of Hiram Abiff (the Temple's architect) by three "ruffians," and the discovery of his burial place through the sprouting of an acacia.

6. See Howard Rollin Patch, *The Other World, According to Descriptions in Medieval Literature* (Cambridge, MA: Harvard University Press, 1950). See also the early work by a scholar later known for his Tibetan studies, W. Y. Evans-Wentz, *The Fairy Faith in Celtic Countries* (Oxford: Oxford University Press, 1911). The fairy folk, it is explained, are the angels who remained neutral in the great war in heaven that concluded with the defeat of Lucifer and his fall to earth. They were condemned to expiate their neutrality by remaining on earth until the Last Judgment.

7. John Keats, *Prometheus Unbound*, act 1.

8. For a profound study, see Henry Corbin, *Creative Imagination in the Sufism of Ibn Arabi*, trans. R. Manheim (Princeton: Princeton/Bollingen, 1969), 184–220.

9. Hosayn Mansur Hallaj (857–922) was crucified for blasphemy. Henry Corbin (*The Man of Light in Iranian Sufism*, 127) reports the fourteenth-century Sufi Semnani as establishing "a connection between the trap into which the Christian dogma of the Incarnation falls by proclaiming the *homoousia* [identity of substance with God the Father] and by affirming that Isa ibn Maryam [Jesus son of Mary] is God, and the mystical intoxication in which such as Hallaj cry out: 'I am God'." Suhrawardi (see chapter 2) was executed for trying to teach the principles of his "Philosophy of Illumination" to young members of the ruling class; the parallel with Socrates is evident.

10. For a translation and analysis, see Antonio T. de Nicolas, *Powers of Imagining: Ignatius de Loyola. A Philosophical Hermeneutic of Imagining through the Collected Works of Ignatius de Loyola, with a Translation* (Albany: State University of New York Press, 1986).

11. See *Baroque Art: The Jesuit Contribution*, ed. R. Wittkower and I. B. Jaffe (New York: Fordham University Press, 1972).

12. Kircher's first description of the magic lantern is in his *Ars Magna Lucis et Umbrae* (Rome: Hermann Scheus, 1646); he developed it further in the second edition of 1671. For an evaluation, see W. A. Wagenaar, "The True Inventor of the Magic Lantern: Kircher, Walgenstein or Huygens?", *Janus* 66 (1979), 193–207.

13. On Swedenborg in his context of time and place, see the collective volume *Emanuel Swedenborg: A Continuing Vision*, ed. R. Larsen (New York: Swedenborg Foundation, 1988).

14. On Swedenborg's initiation and its later repercussions, see Marsha Keith Schuchard, *Why Mrs. Blake Cried: Swedenborg, Blake, and the Sexual Basis of Spiritual Vision* (London: Century, 2006).

15. No less a philosopher than Henry Corbin took them quite seriously: see his *Swedenborg and Esoteric Islam*, trans. Leonard Fox (West Chester, PA: Swedenborg Foundation, 1995).

16. After the model of the Miradj or "night journey" of Mohammed, in which the Prophet was transported by the Angel Gabriel from Mecca to Jerusalem and thence through the seven heavens. The point of his ascent is marked by the Dome of the Rock in Jerusalem, thus the sanctity of the place to Muslims.

17. The Kabbalistic book called *The Greater Holy Assembly*, forming part of the *Zohar*, devotes a chapter to the hair of Macroprosopus (the "Great Face," i.e., the Almighty), and thirteen chapters to his beard.

18. Such as Catholicism (Roman, Anglican, High Episcopalian, etc.), or the Greek and Russian Orthodox churches with their reverence for icons. I here record my gratitude for such an upbringing, which began at the Anglican monastic church of the Cowley Fathers in Oxford and continued as a choirboy in Christ Church Cathedral, in the same city. Half a century later, defying all the trends of the times, there are still cathedrals and churches, even in America, which maintain the traditional rituals, music, and the time-hallowed languages of Latin and Elizabethan English.

19. With consequences mercilessly pinpointed by Robert Bly in *The Sibling Society* (New York: Addison-Wesley, 1996).

CHAPTER 11: *The Pagan Renaissance*

1. The themes of this chapter receive fuller treatment in my book *The Pagan Dream of the Renaissance* (Grand Rapids, MI: Phanes Press, 2002).

2. But see James C. Russell, *The Germanization of Early Medieval Christianity* (Oxford: Oxford University Press, 1996), on how Christianity changed, in the process, into a world-accepting, hierarchical, ethnically reinforcing folk religion.

3. See chapter 4, note 13.

4. This state of order, once almost universal, is evoked in Michell and Rhone, *Twelve-Tribe Nations* (see chapter 3, note 4).

5. Dante was probably on the mark in blaming the popes of his time, and the French king Philip the Fair, who were responsible for crushing the Knights Templar. See *Inferno*, Canto 19, for the pope he encounters in hell, and those who are expected to follow.

6. In the Hindu system, presented in the Puranas, earthly time is subject to a repeating cycle of four ages (*yugas*), of which the Kali Yuga is the last, the shortest, and the worst. Even so, by the traditional reckoning it lasts 432,000 years, a duration that some modern enthusiasts for the concept have sought to modify. For instance, René Guénon allows the Kali Yuga a length of only 6,480 years, and suggests that it began in 4461 B.C. See Guénon, *Formes traditionnelles et cycles cosmiques* (Paris: Gallimard, 1970), 22–24, 48n. The Greek system has four ages of descending merit (Gold, Silver, Bronze, and Iron), between the last of which a fifth "Heroic" age is sometimes interpolated (e.g. in the earliest documented scheme: Hesiod, *Works and Days*, 108–202).

7. Despite the best efforts of Gemistos Plethon (see chapter 1) and Nicolas of Cusa (see chapter 12) to reconcile the churches, as soon as the Eastern representatives returned to Constantinople the union was anulled. The Byzantines had agreed to it chiefly in the hope that the West would save them from the Turks, and this was tragically not to be the case: Constantinople fell in 1453.

8. "Dismal," from *dies mali,* evil or unpropitious days. "Soulless," because the worlds of Darwin, Marx, and Freud have no place for the souls of men or of stars.

9. See Titus Burckhardt, *Siena, City of the Virgin,* trans. M. McD. Brown (Oxford: Oxford University Press, 1960), 65.

10. See Walker, *Spiritual and Demonic Magic from Ficino to Campanella*, 60–63.

11. Ficino was a familiar presence to readers of *Lapis,* which published an extract from a letter of Ficino "On Divine Frenzy," *Lapis* 4 (1997), 57–59; Thomas Moore, "Precious Stones," *Lapis* 7 (1998), 4344; Valery Rees, "Philosophy and Politics: Reconciling the Irreconcilable with Marsilio Ficino," *Lapis* 13 (2001), 71–75.

12. The essential text is Ficino, *De vita coelitus comparanda.* Two English translations exist: *Three Books on Life,* trans. C. Boer (Woodstock, CT: Spring Publications, 1980); *Three Books on Life,* trans. C. V. Kaske & D. J. R. Clark, (Binghamton, NY: Medieval & Renaissance Texts & Studies, 1989).

13. The complete *Picatrix* has not yet been translated into English. A bibliophile's edition of single books in English translation has been announced by the Ouroboros Press in Seattle. There is a scholarly edition: *Picatrix: The Latin Version of the Ghayal al-hakim,* ed. D. E. Pingree (London: Warburg Institute, 1986).

14. This is the subject matter of the first two books ("Natural Magic" and "Celestial Magic") of Henry Cornelius Agrippa, *Three Books of Occult Philosophy.*

15. This is the subject of Agrippa's third book ("Ceremonial Magic") and of the spurious "Fourth Book of Occult Philosophy." English translations: Books 1–3 (published 1651, reprinted Hastings, UK: Chthonios Books, 1986); Book 4 (published 1655, reprinted Gillette, NJ: Heptangle Books, 1985; new translation by Robert Turner, York Beach, ME: Samuel Weiser, 2005).

16. The image is from *Phaedrus,* 251.

CHAPTER 12: *The Philosopher's Dilemma*

1. See chapter 7 on this knowledge or gnosis.

2. St. Catherine of Siena (1347–80) persuaded the pope to return

from decades of exile in Avignon to Rome. Nicholas of Cusa went to Constantinople to attempt the reconciliation of the Eastern and Western churches (see chapter 11).

3. They would face schism in their turn with the appearance of the messianic claimant Sabbatai Sevi (or Zevi) in the year 1666. See Gershom Scholem, *Sabbatai Sevi, the Mystical Messiah,* trans. R. J. Zwi Werblonsky (Princeton: Princeton University Press, 1973).

4. For instance, in Bohemia; see Jean Bérenger, *A History of the Habsburg Empire, 1273–1700,* trans. C. A. Simpson, (London: Longman, 1994), 227.

5. The best all-round study is Christopher McIntosh, *The Rosicrucians: the History, Mythology, and Ritual of an Esoteric Order* (York Beach, ME: Samuel Weiser, 1997). The latest state of Rosicrucian studies is represented by two collective works: *Rosenkreuz als europäisches Phänomen im 17. Jahrhundert* (papers from the 1994 Wolfenbüttel conference in German, English, French; Amsterdam: Bibliotheca Philosophica Hermetica, 2002); *The Rosicrucian Enlightenment Revisited,* ed. R. White (papers from the 1995 Cesky Krumlov and the 1997 Prague conferences; Hudson, NY: Lindisfarne, 1999).

6. Modern English translation: Johann Valentin Andreae, *The Chemical Wedding of Christian Rosenkreuz,* trans. J. Godwin (Grand Rapids, MI: Phanes Press, 1991).

7. Modern English translation: Francesco Colonna, *Hypnerotomachia Poliphili: The Strife of Love in a Dream,* trans. J. Godwin (London: Thames & Hudson, 1999).

8. Dee has become a popular subject nowadays. Still the best all-round study is Peter French, *John Dee: The World of an Elizabethan Magus* (London: Routledge & Kegan Paul, 1976).

9. Paracelsus is less well served in English. A good digest of his obscure thought is Andrew Weeks, *Paracelsus: Speculative*

Theory and the Crisis of the Early Renaissance (Albany: State University of New York Press, 1997).

10. Unlikely to be made redundant is the groundbreaking work of R. W. Evans, *Rudolf II and His World: A Study in Intellectual History, 1576–1612* (Oxford: Oxford University Press, 1972).

11. Ashmole still awaits an interpretive biography, but the groundwork has been done by C. H. Josten in *Elias Ashmole (1617–1692): His Autobiographical and Historical Notes, His Correspondence, and Other Contemporary Sources Relating to His Life and Work,* 5 vols. (Oxford: Clarendon Press, 1967). A stimulating chapter on "Elias Ashmole and the Dee Tradition" appears in Frances A. Yates, *The Rosicrucian Enlightenment* (London: Routledge & Kegan Paul, 1972), 193–205.

12. See Christopher McIntosh, *The Rose Cross and the Age of Reason: Eighteenth-Century Rosicrucianism in Central Europe and its Relationship to the Enlightenment* (Leiden: Brill, 1992).

13. See McIntosh's book for accounts of such powerful figures. The "enlightened despots" referred to include Catherine the Great of Russia, Frederick the Great of Prussia, and Joseph II of Austria.

14. See Schuchard, *Restoring the Temple of Vision.*

15. This has been part of Rosicrucian teaching since Robert Fludd (1574–1637), who explained the cosmos in terms of the intersection of light and dark "pyramids," whose respective expansive and contracting qualities are experienced by us as good and evil; yet metaphysically speaking, they are simply complementary functions of the Creator. For a concise explanation, with Fludd's diagrams, see J. Godwin, *Robert Fludd: Hermetic Philosopher and Surveyor of Two Worlds* (London: Thames & Hudson, 1979, reissued by Phanes Press), 42–51.

16. The majority of the signers of the Declaration of Independence of 1776 (but not Thomas Jefferson) were Freemasons. French Freemasonry included many freethinkers in the tradition of

Diderot and Voltaire, who wished for the downfall of the *ancien régime*. However, this does not make Freemasonry responsible for the "Terror" that ensued, in which Freemasons such as the Duc d'Orléans were guillotined along with the rest.

17. This is not a value judgment. A fragile equilibrium may deserve to be upset. It was on the whole the most conservative elements that were responsible for banning *both* Jesuits and Freemasons. Pope Clement XIV suppressed the Society of Jesus in 1773, yet it was Frederick of Prussia and Catherine of Russia who refused to promulgate the order of suppression, and allowed the Jesuits to continue in their domains.

18. The best established of these are Max Heindel's Rosicrucian Fellowship, H. Spencer Lewis's Ancient and Mystical Order Rosae Crucis (AMORC), R. Swinburne Clymer's Fraternitas Rosae Crucis, Jan van Rijkenborgh's Lectorium Rosicrucianum, and the Societas Roscicruciana in Anglia ("Soc Ros"), which is an order within Freemasonry. See McIntosh, *The Rosy Cross Unveiled*, for an impartial account of these often rival movements.

19. This refers to the tradition that after the Thirty Years' War, the Rosicrucians left Europe and took up residence in Asia. See René Guénon, *The Lord of the World,* trans. A. Cheke (Ellingstring, North Yorkshire, UK: Coombe Springs Press, 1983), 48. On the consequences, see chapter 15.

CHAPTER 13: *Inner Alchemy*

1. The two principal scholars of Christian theosophy today are Antoine Faivre and Arthur Versluis. Among their writings, see especially Faivre's two-part work, *Access to Western Esotericism* (Albany: State University of New York Press, 1994), and *Theosophy, Imagination, Tradition,* trans. C. Rhone (Albany: State University of New York Press, 2000), and Versluis, *Theosophia: Hidden Dimensions of Christianity,* (Hudson, NY:

Lindisfarne, 1994). The academic movement they represent distinguishes "theosophy" and "theosophers" of Boehme's type from "Theosophy" and "Theosophists" stemming from H. P. Blavatsky and the Theosophical Society (see chapter 15). My knowledge of Boehme is drawn from these authors and from John Joseph Stoudt, *Jacob Boehme: His Life and Thought* (New York: Seabury, 1968; originally entitled *Sunrise to Eternity*, 1957).

2. See especially the works of Antoine Faivre cited above.

3. Jacob Boehme, *Aurora,* trans. John Sparrow (London: Watkins, 1914), 103.

4. Basarab Nicolescu, *Science, Meaning, & Evolution: The Cosmology of Jacob Boehme,* trans. R. Baker (New York: Parabola, 1991).

5. These are some of the principles behind the "Transdisciplinary Movement" of which Nicolescu is the founder.

6. This is one of Faivre's six characteristics of esotericism, which have become a sort of canon for the movement to define esotericism and to establish its study as an academic discipline. The first four are "intrinsic" or essential, without which a "discourse" cannot be called esoteric: 1. the idea of correspondence; 2. living nature; 3. imagination and mediation; 4. the experience of transmutation. A further two are "secondary" characteristics, often but not always present: 5. the practice of concordance; and 6. transmission. See his *Theosophy, Imagination, Tradition,* xxi–xxv. The reader may notice the influence of these characteristics on the present work.

7. Boehme was much concerned with Lucifer as the author of the misery of the world. Thus in his terms, ignorance would be "Luciferic" when it opened a door to the activities of this being.

8. On the Behmenist tradition, see Arthur Versluis, *Theosophia* (Hudson, NY: Lindisfarne, 1994) and *Wisdom's Children: a Christian Esoteric Tradition* (Albany: State University of New York Press, 1999). The American branch of the tradition has long attracted local historians and genealogists who have done

invaluable archival research, among whom see Julius Friedrich Sachse, *The German Pietists of Provincial Pennsylvania* (New York: AMS Press, 1970; original ed. 1895).

9. In historical times, alchemy seems to have arisen in the last centuries B.C. in Alexandria and, perhaps independently, in Han dynasty China. See John Read, *Prelude to Chemistry: An Outline of Alchemy, Its Literature and Relationships* (London: G. Bell, 1936), 5.

10. The engraved illustrations of Khunrath's *Amphitheatrum sapientiae aeternae* (1602) are accessible in Stanislas Klossowski de Rola, *The Golden Game: Alchemical Engravings of the Seventeenth Century* (London: Thames & Hudson, 1988), 31–41, but they form only part of a long book, not yet reprinted, much less translated. No easier of access for English language readers is Cesare della Riviera, *Il mondo magico de gli heroi* (1605), ed. J. Evola (n.p.: Edizioni Arktos, 1982); but much of its substance is included, in more comprehensible form, in Julius Evola's *The Hermetic Tradition: Symbols & Teachings of the Royal Art,* trans. E. E. Rehmus, (Rochester, VT: Inner Traditions, 1995). For Vaughan, see *The Works of Thomas Vaughan, Mystic and Alchemist (Eugenius Philalethes),* ed. A. E. Waite (New Hyde Park, NY: University Books, 1968).

11. This description owes much to my reading of the Gruppo di Ur's work (see chapter 1, note 8).

12. This expression comes from the forgotten multifaceted genius Charles Henry (1859–1926), who is quoted as saying: "Death is merely a physiochemical event of no importance," and adding, "it is only after my death that I will begin to amuse myself seriously." Quoted in Godwin, *Music and the Occult,* 117.

13. In C. G. Jung, *Collected Works*, trans. R. F. C. Hull, (Princeton: Princeton/Bollingen, 1960–76). The relevant volumes are 12, *Psychology and Alchemy;* 13, *Alchemical Studies;* and 14, *Mysterium Coniunctionis.*

14. See Fulcanelli, *Le Mystère des Cathédrales: Esoteric Interpretation of the Hermetic Symbols of the Great Work*, trans. M. Sworder (London: Neville Spearman, 1971), and *The Dwellings of the Philosophers*, trans. B. Donvez and L. Perrin (Boulder, CO: Archive Press, 1999).

15. See Frater Albertus, *The Alchemist's Handbook: Manual for Practical Laboratory Alchemy* (New York: Samuel Weiser, 1974); Jean Dubuis' work was accessible through The Philosophers of Nature and their journal *The Stone*, now ceased.

16. For a practical introduction to spagyric alchemy in the tradition of Frater Albertus and Dubuis, see Mark Stavish, *The Path of Alchemy: Energetic Healing and the World of Natural Magic* (Woodbury, MN: Llewellyn, 2006).

17. See J. Godwin, "Mentalism and the Cosmological Fallacy," *Alexandria: The Journal of the Western Cosmological Traditions* 3 (1993), 195–204, and the criticisms of Michael Hornum, "Knowledge, Reason, and Ethics: A Neoplatonic Perspective," *Alexandria* 4 (1995), 131–55. My mentalistic position is not based on any academic training in philosophy, but on the common-sense teachings of Paul Brunton, especially his two-part work *The Hidden Teaching Beyond Yoga* (New York: Dutton, 1941), and *The Wisdom of the Overself* (New York: Dutton, 1943). Since discovering Brunton's works in the 1960s I have found no reason to discard their philosophical principles.

CHAPTER 14: *The Religion of Art*

1. Thus the *Shorter Oxford Dictionary*. The word must have carried much the same charge as "fundamentalism" does today.

2. Among them one could list the English Gothic novel (Ann Radcliffe, Matthew Lewis); the "Gothick" revival in architecture, especially as practiced by Horace Walpole at Strawberry Hill and by William Beckford at Fonthill Abbey (now col-

lapsed); Walter Scott's *Ivanhoe*; the German school of painters called the Nazarenes; the medievalism of the Biedermeier period, e.g., Schloss Hohenschwangau, decorated by Moritz von Schwind; then on to the Pre-Raphaelites, Victor Hugo's *Notre Dame de Paris,* Tennyson's *Idylls of the King,* Viollet le Duc's restorations, the architecture favored by the Oxford Movement, etc.

3. This idea was of signal importance to the worldviews of the Traditionalists, especially René Guénon and Julius Evola. See two books first published in 1929: Guénon's *Spiritual Authority and Temporal Power,* trans. Henry D. Fohr (Ghent, NY: Sophia Perennis, 2004) and *The Esoterism of Dante,* trans. Henry D. Fohr (Ghent, NY: Sophia Perennis, 2005). See also Evola's *The Mystery of the Grail,* trans. G. Stucco (Rochester, VT: Inner Traditions, 1997).

4. See Johann Wolfgang von Goethe, "Von deutscher Baukunst," in *Sämtliche Werke* (Frankfurt a.M., Deutsche Klassiker Verlag, 1998), 18:110–18.

5. This is not my flippant opinion, but the considered verdict of one of the Muse's most faithful companions, the late British poet Kathleen Raine. In her obituary for *The Tablet* of fellow-poet David Gascoyne (December 2001), she wrote that the last real poet of the twentieth century had now departed.

6. Some titles: Novalis, *The Disciples at Saïs; The Blue Flower*; E. T. A. Hoffmann, *The Golden Pot*; Gérard de Nerval, *Aurélia*; Honoré de Balzac, *Séraphîta, Louis Lucas*; George Sand, *Consuélo, The Countess of Rudolstadt*; Edward Bulwer-Lytton, *Zanoni: A Strange Story.*

7. To these should be added the overdue respect paid to Haydn in his later years, especially after *The Creation* (1804), which was seen by some critics as evidence of the divinely creative nature of the composer, and by others compared with the Gothic cathedrals themselves. See Michael Embach and J. Godwin, *J. F. H. von Dalberg, 1760–1812: Schriftsteller, Musiker, Domherr*

(Mainz: Gesellschaft für mittelrheinische Kirchengeschichte, 1998), 336–38.

8. The one Buddhist among the Traditionalist group, Marco Pallis, had a lifelong love of Wagner's music dramas, expressed in his very last article, "Hands Off Wagner!" in *Temenos* 5 (1984), 81–88.

9. H. C. Robbins Landon, *1791: Mozart's Last Year* (London: Thames & Hudson, 1988), 10.

CHAPTER 15: *Wise Men from the East*

1. See chapter 12, note 19.

2. Hence the two volumes of her first book, *Isis Unveiled* (New York, 1877), were subtitled *Science* and *Theology*. Writings about Blavatsky were long divided between hagiographies from within the Theosophical movement, and hatchet jobs from outside it, the latter often at a puerile level that would not be tolerated in the case of historical and literary figures of far less significance. At last in 1985, with the foundation of the journal *Theosophical History* by Leslie Price (refounded by James A. Santucci with the New Series, 1990), a forum opened for impartial research on the Theosophical movement. The new trend is evident in Nicholas Goodrick-Clarke's introduction to his anthology *Helena Blavatsky* (Berkeley: North Atlantic, 2004; Western Esoteric Masters series).

3. See James A. Santucci, "Does Theosophy Exist in the Theosophical Society?" in *Mélanges offerts à Antoine Faivre*, 471–89.

4. On this as on all points of biographical fact, see Boris de Zirkoff's "Chronological Survey," which prefaces most volumes of *Blavatsky's Collected Writings* (Wheaton, IL: Theosophical Publishing House, 1966–91).

5. The Mahatmas' versions of the teachings are in *The Mahatma Letters to A. P. Sinnett* (New York: Frederick P. Stokes, 1924 and reissues). Blavatsky enlarged greatly on them in *The Secret Doctrine* and in her essays.

6. A short book dedicated to presenting the evidence for this is David Reigle, *The Books of Kiu-Te, or The Tibetan Buddhist Tantras: A Preliminary Analysis* (San Diego: Wizards Bookshelf, 1983).

7. K. Paul Johnson, *The Masters Revealed: Madame Blavatsky and the Myth of the Great White Lodge* (Albany: State University of New York Press, 1994).

8. See Christopher Isherwood, *Ramakrishna and His Disciples* (New York: Simon & Schuster, 1965).

9. Romain Rolland, *The Life of Ramakrishna* and *The Life of Vivekananda and the Universal Gospel* (both published at Almora, India: Advaita Ashrama, 1931).

10. See Arthur Osborne, *Ramana Maharshi and the Path of Self-Knowledge* (London: Rider, 1970).

11. See *Maha-Yoga or The Upanishadic Lore in the Light of the Teachings of Bhagavan Sri Ramana, by "Who"* (Tiruvannamalai, India: Sri Ramanasramam, n.d.)

12. If Ramana's renunciation of the world is thought too impractical an example, an alternative model might be his contemporary Atmananda (Krishna Menon, 1883–1959) who taught the Advaitic philosophy while holding a job as district superintendent of police. See Nitya Tripta, *Notes on Spiritual Discourses of Sree Atmananda (of Trivandrum), 1950–1959* (Trivandrum, India: Reddiar Press, 1963).

13. See especially his comparative work, *Shiva and Dionysus,* trans. K. F. Hurry (Rochester, VT: Inner Traditions, 1984), and his critique of the modern West, *While the Gods Play,* trans. B. Bailey et al. (Rochester, VT: Inner Traditions, 1987).

14. Material on and by Bennett is scattered in rare journals, but some of it is gathered in J. Godwin, *The Theosophical Enlightenment* (Albany: State University of New York Press, 1994), 369–76.

15. See especially Suzuki's *Zen and Japanese Culture* (New York: Pantheon/Bollingen, 1959), and the three volumes of *Essays in Zen Buddhism* (London: Rider, 1949–53).

16. Among a copious literature, see the work of an early German convert, Lama Anagarika Govinda, *The Way of the White Clouds* (London: Hutchinson, 1966), and, for the Dzogchen school, Namkhai Norbu, *The Crystal and the Way of Light*.

17. The expression "personal equation" was a favorite of Julius Evola (1898–1974), perhaps influenced by his early training as an engineer. It suggests that each person comes into the world with a unique character and program, which it is the duty of a lifetime to "solve."

CHAPTER 16: *The End of the Thread?*

1. Blavatsky did not understand race in modern terms, but as the coming into incarnation of humans with a new set of physical and spiritual characteristics. For a brief summary, see Blavatsky, *The Secret Doctrine,* 1:xliii.

2. These are the closing words of H. P. Blavatsky, *The Key to Theosophy* (London: Theosophical Publishing Co., 1889), 307.

3. See chapter 12, note 18.

4. Transpersonal psychology, a loosely defined movement, is most closely associated with the name of Roberto Assagioli, the founder of Psychosynthesis, who was a disciple of a Tibetan Mahatma channeled by Alice A. Bailey.

5. This is amply demonstrated by Wouter J. Hanegraaff in his

seminal book, *New Age Religion and Western Culture: Esotericism in the Mirror of Secular Thought* (Leiden: E. J. Brill, 1996).

6. Official science, preferring the chimera of progress to the wisdom of its own forefathers, missed the boat after World War I. Until then, psychical research and the investigation of mediumship had occupied scientists of the eminence of John Logie Baird, Sir William Barrett, Sir William Crookes, Camille Flammarion, William James, Sir Oliver Lodge, Cesare Lombroso, Charles Richet, and Alfred Russel Wallace.

7. On the Hindu doctrine of the *yugas*, see chapter 11, note 6. The only general study of the Traditionalists, or "Perennialists" as they are sometimes called, is Mark Sedgwick, *Against the Modern World: Traditionalism and the Secret Intellectual History of the Twentieth Century* (Oxford: Oxford University Press, 2004). For a measured approach to the most influential of them, see Robin Waterfield, *René Guénon and the Future of the West* (n.p.: Crucible, 1987). Readers of Spanish should consult the many writings of Federico González, especially his *Esoterismo siglo XXI: En torno a René Guénon* (Seville: Muñoz Moya Editores, 2000) and the journal *Symbolos,* which he has edited since 1990.

8. See Guénon's *The Reign of Quantity and the Signs of the Times,* trans. Lord Northbourne (London: Luzac, 1953), especially the chapter on "The Degeneration of Coinage."

9. This was the conclusion of Evola's late book (1961), *Cavalcare la tigre;* English translation by J. Godwin and C. Fontana, *Ride the Tiger: A Survival Manual for Aristocrats of the Soul* (Rochester, VT: Inner Traditions, 2003).

10. For an evaluation of this movement by a prominent historian of Freemasonry and Christian philosopher, see R. A. Gilbert, *Casting the First Stone: The Hypocrisy of Religious Fundamentalism and Its Threat to Society,* (Shaftesbury, Dorset, UK: Element, 1993).

11. See the examples of invective by Peter Dawkins and others collected in Richard Milton's *Shattering the Myth of Darwinism* (Rochester, VT: Park Street Press, 2000), or the infamous review of Rupert Sheldrake's *A New Science of Life* in *Nature*, 293 (5830), 245–56, entitled "A Book for Burning?"

12. See the analysis of the Hermetic roots of the U.S. in Hoeller, *Freedom: Alchemy for a Voluntary Society*; also in Robert Hieronimus, *America's Secret Destiny: Spiritual Vision and the Founding of a Nation* (Rochester, VT: Destiny, 1989).

13. William Blake's term for the angry, personal God; see his poem "When Klopstock England defied."

Index

QUEST BOOKS

encourages open-minded inquiry into
world religions, philosophy, science, and the arts
in order to understand the wisdom of the ages,
respect the unity of all life, and help people explore
individual spiritual self-transformation.

Its publications are generously supported by
The Kern Foundation,
a trust committed to Theosophical education.

Quest Books is the imprint of
the Theosophical Publishing House,
a division of the Theosophical Society in America.
For information about programs, literature,
on-line study, membership benefits, and international centers,
see www.theosophical.org
or call 800-669-1571 or (outside the U.S.) 630-668-1571.

Related Quest Titles

Gnosticism, by Stephan A. Hoeller

Hidden Wisdom, by Richard Smoley and Jay Kinney

Isis Unveiled: by H. P. Blavatsky

Jesus Christ: Sun of God, by David Fideler

To order books or a complete Quest catalog,
call 800-669-9425 or (outside the U.S.) 630-665-0130.